BECAUSE OF MY
HORSE

Praise for *Because of my Horse*

"Cathy Huddleston has created a heart-wrenching, heartwarming memoir to connect all the frayed pieces of your soul. Her beautifully told stories bind together a life to inspire, reveal, and entreat any reader to look deeper, see further, and feel from a place of profound vulnerability and authenticity. You won't be disappointed. I didn't want the book to end. I wanted to stay with Cathy even longer 'because of her horses' but also because of her wonderful storytelling."

–Stacey Simmons, PhD, author of *The Queen's Path: A Revolutionary Guide to Women's Empowerment and Sovereignty*

"As a trauma psychologist for thirty plus years, I can honestly say that *Because of My Horse* reveals profound insights about trauma, healing, and the deep bonds between humans and animals. This is a pioneering and thoroughly engaging exploration of how the relationships between horses and humans can guide us back to our own innate wisdom and capacity for healing. Written with warmth and unflinching honesty, it's as enjoyable as it is illuminating. A must read for anyone looking to better understand the road to resilience and connection."

–Rebecca Bailey, PhD, Polyvagal Equine Institute

"Cathy Huddleston is a teacher profoundly in tune with her students, a perpetually curious student, a passionate friend of both humans and horses, and woman who walks a spiritual path. She shares her life stories of challenges, traumas, and realities that could cripple a girl emotionally, physically, and mentally. However, she doesn't write from darkness to heal herself. Instead, she weaves a narrative of secrets with the light of awareness and compassion gained from a loving family, friends, lovers, and her beloved horses.

Cathy offers insight gained from an unconditional love realized by being innocently open-hearted and devoted to her horses. These are tender and intimate stories. But more revealing is witnessing Cathy's innate understanding of true power, forgiveness, and grace which began with lessons from her dad and a pony named Franco."

–Karen Head, M.Ed., facilitator and founder of Equinection LLC

"What you have in your hand is a raw, unabridged journey through a landscape of sexual trauma and its impacts. Embrace the journey as Cathy finds a new way of being in her own body while showing us a new way of being with horses, while lifting the yoke of trauma that has bound her since childhood. Honor the way the horses showed up for her, again and again, walking beside her and sometimes carrying her through life.

You will laugh, you will cry, you will be emboldened with anger and will find your voice through this coming-of-age memoir. You will also develop a deeper understanding of the nature and impacts of trauma through the eyes of an innocent girl, who emerges as a vibrant and beautiful woman, able to see herself as her guides, the horses, have seen her all along; as strong, gentle, loving, two-legged, now living life with open arms and an open heart."

–Melanie Dallas, LPC, equine facilitated therapist practitioner

"This book is a really in-depth and hard look into the soul of someone I admire greatly. Cathy holds nothing back of herself, laying it all out there for everyone to see. I laughed, cried, and felt hope along with her as she went through a journey that many could not have completed. Cathy has been a teacher, an inspiration, and a friend to me when I needed that in my life. I truly would not be the man I am today without her."

–Brad Altherr, veteran

"While all of our journeys are unique, this author's unflinching retelling of hers has the power to help lead so many of us in the direction of healing. And that, through the most gifted healers among us — horses."

–David Sonatore, LCSW, author and co-founder of The Equus Effect

Learning to
Ride Through
Life with Courage
and Resilience

BECAUSE OF MY
HORSE

Catherine Huddleston

This book reflects the author's recollections of experiences over time. Some names and characteristics have been changed, some events have been compressed, and some dialogue has been recreated.

Published by Ochiltree Press

To contact the author about speaking or ordering books in bulk, visit www.cathyhuddleston.com

Edited by Katie Mather
Book design by Christy Day, ConstellationBookServices.com
Author photo credit: Jessica Guadagnoli, photographer

ISBN (paperback): 979-8-9918325-0-2
ISBN (ebook): 979-8-9918325-1-9

Library of Congress Control Number: 2024924602

Printed in the United States of America

AUTHOR'S NOTE

Most chapter titles are named after a specific horse. Each of these horses were anchor points in my life during the events of the chapter. My beloved horses helped me and taught me along the way. They provided a sanctuary for my heart, a safe place to return to whenever I needed. They held me within their herd figuratively and literally, granting me the safety and security I needed to move from surviving to thriving. All because of my horse.

Content Warning

The content of this book may be emotionally challenging. It contains graphic descriptions of abuse, sexual assault, animal death, and homophobia and may not be suitable for young readers.

INTRODUCTION

YOU DON'T KNOW ME YET. I'm a fierce cowgirl who grew into a skilled horsewoman and facilitator. I came into the world a vibrant being. When my light began to shine, it glistened with the colors of the rainbow. Over time my life was shaded by trauma, and like so many survivors, my once vibrant rainbow was dulled.

Today I am a facilitator of self-empowerment and healing through engagement with horses. Simply put, I bring horses and people together in workshops where horses model and embody the knowledge of the herd.

I am often described as a wounded healer. A woman held together by the knitted scars of trauma—but I am also so much more, just like you. I'm choosing to tell my story now because there is healing and power in finding our voices, and I want to invite you to join the chorus to empower change. We must have the hard conversations and embrace sitting in discomfort to get to the other side.

I hope that you find learning in these pages. That you find tears, laughter, and feel all the feels as you read about my journey. I am but a single drop in the sea of stories of life, but my story matters, and so does yours!

Cathy

FRANCO

AGED TWO AND A HALF, I successfully manifested my very first pony, Franco. I came into this world wanting—needing—horses in my life. I loved horses. *Loved* them! My dad was the county social worker and had grown up in the area. Everyone knew my father in our community of two thousand or so people. He had grown up just across the state line in Towner, Colorado, the oldest child in a family who owned the local mercantile store. Think *Little House on the Prairie* mixed with *Fried Green Tomatoes*.

He worked in the store as a kid all the way up to adulthood and was forced to dress nicely, which he hated, forced to wear wool knickers, a vest, a button down shirt, and a flat hat. He was expected to stand out when all he wanted to do was fit in. When I came along, he was living the lifestyle he had desired as a kid: simple, wearing overalls all day and having a garden, where he could milk goats, and keep rabbits and chickens. Ironically, this made us stand out as a family and not fit in.

Because of Dad's role in the community, almost everyone crossed paths with him at some point. One day when I was two and a half, a local rancher walked into his office and said, "Howard, that girl of yours needs a pony. These folks dropped one off at my place several years ago, paid one month's board, and haven't been back. So, if you can catch the little son of a bitch, you can have him for that girl."

The following Saturday, my big brother, Jerry, and my dad left in the morning and by evening I was levitating with excitement. When I heard the dogs barking their familiar alert to Dad's arrival home, I raced up the stairs and out the door.

Dad and Jerry were pulling up in our 1956 pickup, both grinning ear to ear and filthy, covered in western Kansas dust and dried sweat. In the back of the truck bed, lined with old wooden and weathered stock racks, was my pony. He looked anxious with big brown eyes, alert ears and turning in different directions only to stop and whinny as he would peek out on different sides. Dad smiled and waved as Mom grabbed my hand to stop me from running in front of the pickup. I could hardly breathe I was so desperate to see my pony.

Dad and Jerry got out, went around to the back, and lowered the tailgate. As Dad lifted the gate on the stock rack, Jerry slipped in and grabbed my pony. Out they came and there he was, a golden caramel-colored pony with the thickest flaxen mane and tail. He was the most beautiful thing I'd ever seen. It was instantaneous love for me.

I named him Franco after my favorite food at the time, Franco-American SpaghettiOs. It was love at first sight. He was a yearling when he was dropped off at the ranch, now around five years old, so he hadn't been trained. My dad, being who he was and believing in experiential life lessons, turned me loose. Franco was my first horse; my first equine teacher, the first horse I trained, and my very first equine partner.

I don't remember all the details of our journey together, just specific moments and adventures. I remember how his coat felt when I would stroke it and how he smelled of dirt and horse when I would bury my face in his neck. I remember just sitting on him bareback as he would wander and graze, and feeling content and safe as if being held in the warmth of the universe.

I remember learning how to sit his trot. One day, I walked into our house and excitedly dragged my parents outside. They *had* to see what I had accomplished. I was so proud! I lined my folks up at the fence and, dressed in a lime green metallic cowboy hat, vest, and chinks ordered from the *Sears and Roebuck* catalog, marched off across the paddock to catch my steed. There Franco was, my gorgeous chestnut pony with a flaxen mane and tail, red halter, his lead rope dragging as he grazed, waiting for me to come back. I caught him and marched us across to the nearest fence with a confidence I wore like a golden cape. We had done this numerous times; I believe I was age three at that point.

I lined him up along the fence, pushing his hindquarters as close as I could to the fence rail. Then I climbed atop the fence and scooted forward until I reached his back. Over I slid onto my mighty and fierce mount, lead rope in hand, and then off we went at a walk. I began to kick, and I'm sure we looked like a Thelwell cartoon without a saddle, with me kicking as hard as I could until eventually my pony gave in and moved to a trot. I grabbed his mane; two strides later, the mane slipped from my hands as I began to bounce backward. Five strides in and I was on his croup. Six strides: I was bouncing off his rump toward the ground and then *thud*. Up I jumped, dusted myself off, and with determination, stomped across the pen to capture my pony and try again. I was so very proud of myself and excited.

Eventually, my folks got me a saddle and bridle. My skills improved, and our adventures broadened. Growing up in a small town in Middle of Nowhere, Western Kansas meant my adventures were spread county-wide. As Franco and I expanded our partnership we ventured further out from home. We resided in town on a large lot, and my pony lived in the backyard. He was always there in those early years, and it was awesome! I was the neighborhood kid with a pony and my yard was the fun place to play.

We had a giant dirt pile from the root cellar my dad had dug. Dad also built us a treehouse, which included a bridge across to another tree where he'd built steps to climb up into it. That bridge saw many kids, leading to times when we sat up there shouting raunchy songs we'd learned at the tops of our lungs, profanity included. There was a garden below where we pulled carrots from the dirt, some for Franco and some we just ate. We had chickens and rabbits and dogs, storage sheds and playhouses, and the freedom to roam and explore. I had no fear and was as fierce and confident as they came.

As a kid, I was a monkey; I loved climbing, and I didn't limit it to my treehouse. I grew up in a basement house that resembled a roof on top of about a three-foot wall. We had an entrance that looked like any regular front entrance, but ours immediately led to stairs down into the house. The entrance was enclosed with a separate roof from the house and was ten or so feet above ground level; the house's roof peaked at about two feet higher than the porch where it tied into the porch roof.

I loved climbing and playing on our roof. It was, to my imagination, a pirate ship, and the chimney was the mast. So many adventures were had on that roof, and as my climbing skills improved, I began to scale everything I could find. We had a separate garage, and eventually, I managed to leap the four-foot gap and walkway between the garage and house. I cannot imagine the sound all us kids made thundering across the roof as we fought imaginary pirates or leaped from the garage ship to board the house ship.

Around kindergarten age I went through a clean phase. I had to be in clean clothes all the time. My mom tolerated my constant wardrobe switches for a short while but reached a point where she eventually forbade me from changing during the day. I'm sure the amount of laundry was quite excessive, as I would change outfits four to five times a day. I argued and lost but didn't give up, and so the great sneak-and-change plot was hatched. So determined was I to wear only squeaky-clean clothes, I planned the best way to change and not get caught. I would act normal, and when it was time to change, I would simply go in the house for a drink or bathroom break. When my mom wasn't looking, I'd sneak in and out of my room with articles of clothing hidden under my shirt or bundled with toys, which I would take to change into.

I discovered on my first attempt that I couldn't take a whole outfit as it was too noticeable, so I began taking a few items at a time. I quickly developed a system and a hiding place. Up on the roof I would go where I couldn't be seen by Mom, and in between the porch and house roof was the perfect hiding place for my clean outfits to change into and for me to stash the dirty clothes. This went on for several days quite successfully. I think my mom thought her declaration had worked as there wasn't a pile of clothes in the laundry. However, lo and behold, several days later the phone rang. My mom answered. It was the neighbor across the street on the corner, who asked whether my mom knew I was on the roof buck-ass naked. Out came mom to see her daughter on the roof, a little blond-haired, blue-eyed girl with a very tan body in nothing but a pair of white underwear. She had caught me in the middle of one of my outfit changes. And so, the jig was up, and my clean clothes phase came to an end.

As I developed my training skills, I taught my pony how to rear on command like the Lone Ranger. The neighbor boy and I would play "Cowboys and Indians" on our block.

My house was Indian territory, and the house next door was designated the cowboy fort house; it had the perfect porch for the job, with stairs up to the main entrance and a three-foot-high wall around the front of it. The cowboys could hide and then pop out and shoot at me as I thundered by on Franco, whoopin' and hollerin' and pretending to shoot my bow and arrows at them. I would gallop back around to my house, where there was a single cable enclosing the front yard. Franco would slide to a stop and then rear on command as I would dive off of him and roll under the cable into the yard and hide. Franco would immediately start grazing unbothered, and before long, off we would go again. It's a miracle I didn't decapitate myself.

One day, my dad came home with a cart-and-pony harness. He taught me how to tack up Franco with the harness and attach the cart, and Franco learned to drive and pull the cart. I had so much fun learning how to drive. We would go all over town with the cart to give rides. People would always point and wave as we would trot by, and Franco would perk up, ears forward and knees higher as if showing off for the spectators. Eventually, the rearing turned into a tool for that clever pony, and he would begin to rear while pulling the cart if we were out past feeding time! I never knew how to counter that behavior. Frankly, it gave me butterflies in my stomach, so we would turn and head for the barn when he gave me that signal. His clock always won, and he never reared while driving except for that specific reason. Honestly, it's tough to win over someone's dinner time.

He and I had such adventures. He was my best friend, and I was his girl. I shared him with the neighborhood kids and my friends, which, at best, he tolerated. I remember one incident when a boy came over to play. We were out with Franco, and Tommy, a smart aleck kid from down the street thinking he was being funny, walked up behind Franco and slapped him on the ass as hard as he could while Franco was eating. That pony responded by kicking Tommy square in the acorns; he dropped to his knees with a loud ooooffff and then a small squeak as he collapsed to the ground red-faced and crying. To this day, I don't know why he did that or whether he learned his lesson. But a clear lesson in boundaries was taught to us both that day, along with a strong reminder to think before acting.

The first time I remember a stranger touching me inappropriately was a neighborhood boy who was older. We were playing hide-and-seek at a neighbor's house, and he suggested we hide together under the porch. It was just past dusk and the street lights turned on with that familiar loud buzzing sound. He asked to see my undercarriage and, in turn, he'd show me his.

The premise was to see how different our body parts were. I knew him and didn't feel afraid, so I agreed because I, too, was curious. I grew up with livestock and had been educated on reproduction. I knew the difference between male and female genitalia, but who was I to question a boy? I was also unsure how to get away without hurting his feelings—clearly cultural programming was already in place. That was the first time I remember a male touching me, holding me down, and penetrating me.

I remember how the damp ground under the porch smelled that night all musty and damp. I remember how the streetlights reflected through the lattice creating patterns on the ground and across his body. I remember the sharp pain when he forcefully entered me, my breath catching and wincing. How his breathing changed to panting as he thrust inside of me and I could feel and smell the blood as it came from inside my little body onto the ground below me.

I remember how he smelled as he began to sweat. I remember the tears running out of the corner of my eyes, wanting to be anywhere else. Feeling afraid and powerless, numb and confused, hearing voices far away talking and laughing in the neighborhood. I felt helpless and defeated. Where was the safety I had experienced with my Franco? Why couldn't I be the ferocious girl on that pony in this moment, set a boundary, and ride away?

Afterward he told me that it was my fault, that I'd agreed to it, and to tell no one because I would get in really big trouble. Ashamed and afraid, I pulled up my underwear and shorts over the blood. I ran home and straight to the bathroom, where I removed my bloody underwear and threw them away, hiding them in a rolled-up cardboard toilet paper roll at the bottom of the waste bin terrified my parents would find out and I'd get in trouble. The experience was physically painful. I was six years old, and truly had no concept of what I was going along with. That is when the secret-keeping began, and shame and guilt started to creep in through the cracks of my identity and self-esteem.

I look back after years of therapy with acceptance and forgiveness but the pangs of guilt still linger. I remember what six-years-old looks like, a small blonde-haired, blue-eyed child with curiosity in her eyes that turned to fear and shame after one night of violence against a trusting heart and body. I try to shift my perspective to empathy and understanding for myself whenever those memories come to visit. It took years to reach this mindset, and sometimes that in itself really pisses me off. The emotional complexity of that single moment in my life changed me forever and that little girl, my six-year-old self, didn't deserve it.

I ran home that night and told no one. I went to Franco the next day and cried into his mane. He stood with me, breathed with me, and was a soft shoulder to lean into. He was safe, always. I knew enough to never be alone with that neighbor boy again. I did, however, pretend to be a warrior on my mighty steed more frequently after that night as a rage within began to surface.

Franco seemed to encourage and embrace my ferocity. It's interesting to look back and recognize the moment when I chose to become invisible in parts of my life, invisible to humans I wasn't sure about or didn't trust, all of whom were male. My dad was safe, and that was conflicting information for me early on. My innate survival programming told me to be careful around boys who tried to talk me into anything, but for men…no alarm bells went off, they were supposed to be safe like my Dad and brothers.

As a young girl in the 1970s, I was exposed to a certain culture. Everything portrayed on TV and modeled in my community implied that women were *for* men. Women dressed to please men, and cooked and cleaned for men, while men made the decisions for the family and wife. Women didn't have careers other than nurse or secretary. This culture didn't match what was taught in my home. My dad told me I could be and do *anything*, a concept encouraged throughout my upbringing. What I didn't know was that my freedom at home did not extend into the wider world—I needed to protect myself…and I didn't know how.

Life lessons I acquired with Franco certainly stand out in my mind, like the day I discovered barrel racing at a rodeo. I decided I really wanted a crop like the big girls had when they would run a barrel pattern. I watched those girls and realized they used the crop to get their horses to go faster by spanking the horses' backside. I begged and begged, and Dad finally gave in and got me one, though he instructed me to only use it on my boot to make noise, never on my pony. I excitedly agreed, assuming I'd won the battle by getting my crop. I believed myself to be quite clever and only used the crop on my boot whenever Dad watched. When I would go to the crop, Franco would gallop faster. But fast was all I could think about at the time. So, when I thought Dad wasn't looking, I spanked my pony right on the rear.

Let me tell you, it worked. He shot off like a rocket. It

was awesome! I had no concept at such a young age that my pony was going so fast because I'd inflicted pain on him. It didn't take long before I forgot about Dad watching and got caught. I was yanked off my pony in one fell swoop, crop in hand. I don't remember thinking *Uh-oh*, but I knew I was in trouble, that I had crossed a line on a deeper level because I was hiding my actions, and that's never good. I remember Dad asking if I knew I was causing my pony pain. I didn't answer; just stood there defiantly staring up at him, my heart pounding in my ears, with squinty, hot eyes leering back. He talked for a while as I stood with my arms crossed. I do not remember what was said except that I needed to know what it felt like to be my pony, getting the crop.

That statement got my attention.

He didn't leave welts; the punishment wasn't meant to be abusive or was done out of anger. But he did give me several swats across the backside to ensure I had experienced the crop as Franco had. Through my pants I felt the sting and fire as it awoke my nerve endings. It seemed as if my backside burst into flames with sensation and stinging. He believed I needed to know both sides of the experience, and it worked. That day, I came to respect the power of my actions toward my pony. I had unknowingly become the abuser to my beloved Franco.

I never used that crop on Franco again, and that lesson stayed with me. For every horse I've ever ridden throughout my career, my whip or crop has been utilized as a tool for communication, not a weapon. A way to provide guidance to create a boundary or touch in a place I can't reach with my hand or heel. A tool used to enhance communication and trust in partnership.

I had one more lesson similar to the crop with Franco that I remember vividly, and that involved the bit. All those westerns I watched on TV taught me to yank my horse around dramatically while steering him. Every time one of those actors got on, they seemed to yank the reins as hard as they could; they yanked their horse left, yanked them right, and even yanked them to a stop. I watched and learned as if, in my mind, I was training to be a cowboy.

Dad and I would talk about how I was using my hands, how all that yanking must have felt to my pony with that bit stuck behind his teeth and over his tongue creating pain and pressure with every pull, but I didn't listen yet again. After all, he couldn't possibly be right. Dad was no cowboy. Those cowboys on TV knew what they were doing, and they had to be right.

I remember several talks from Dad about how yanking the reins meant painfully yanking on my pony's mouth, and his "or else." In other words, the consequences I'd face if I didn't listen. But again, I knew better. I started watching for Dad whenever I'd ride and snuck in the yanking when I thought I was alone. And, of course, again, I got caught, and his "or else" happened. Off I came, and I got a talkin' to, but this time, he was standing there with baling twine in his hand. Before I knew what was happening, he told me to place the twine in my mouth like a bit and then stood behind me like he was holding the reins. My hands were to stay at my sides, and he demonstrated what it felt like to be yanked on from the mouth. I only remember how the twine felt prickly and made the corners of my mouth sore. What stands out the most from this lesson was the shame I felt for my actions.

Looking back, I know Dad was careful; no cuts or abrasions in the corners of my mouth like I know happens to horses who receive such treatment, but he did leave an important impression via all that shame and discomfort. It is a fine line, distinguishing behaviors and actions modeled by humans. I was a child seeking knowledge about becoming a cowgirl. I embraced what I saw and what was accepted, instead of honoring words. I came to learn about violence against others through violence, not uncommon for many of us. I learned empathy for my pony and the pain I had inflicted upon him, much like the pain I experienced during my assault, was how I gained empathy. Two experience-based lessons in which I embodied learning, and it changed me for a lifetime for the better.

Franco and I were inseparable, but I was growing physically, which meant only one thing: I would soon outgrow my pony. I swore to keep him forever. He stayed with me for a few more years, providing adventures for my friends, but in time, we all outgrew him. I ultimately gave him to my cousin's two boys in central Kansas. Their parents were not fond of that pony or his independence and unique training, but one of the boys loved and rode him, dreaming of becoming a cowboy. That boy did, in fact, grow up to become a real cowboy, a cattle rancher, husband, and father. Franco empowered two young people who went on to live out their horse dreams.

WENDY

I DON'T REMEMBER HOW we learned Wendy was for sale. I still had Franco, but it was time to go up a size in mounts. She was a cob-sized mare that had raised several girls one town south of my hometown in Western Kansas. I went to see her, and, just like it had been with Franco, it was love at first sight. But she was nothing like Franco. Wendy was motherly, quiet, steady, and gentle. She was solid brown while Franco was a flashy chestnut with a flaxen mane and tail—so very different, and I loved her.

When she came home, my horses no longer lived in my backyard. We had leased a pasture and barns two miles from our house and shared the property with a family friend and her daughters. Her girls were older than me, and I followed the youngest around like a big sister. Our families were close, sharing meals often. Their mom and my dad shared the love of gardening, milk goats, and garage sales.

Wendy was also nothing like Franco in movement. Her gaits were controlled and easy, whereas Franco was like riding a rocket, which I'd loved at the time. He drove hard from behind and would thunder across the plains at a gallop. Wendy just loped gently and steadily. It took a while for me to adapt to her. How could I continue my life of adventure with such a gentle and steady partner? What trouble could we possibly drum up? What could I possibly learn from such a quiet mount?

Much, it turned out. What she gifted me was steadiness from a master teacher. No matter what I thought or demanded she give, nothing advanced until she deemed me ready for more, no matter how hard I pushed. Looking back, I've come to realize that she forced me to learn to move with her and find balance in myself, to find self-carriage, a different kind of quiet partnership. As we came together, and my riding skills progressed, she offered me more animated movement. Lo and behold, I began to develop confidence in my ability to simply and quietly ride with my horse, my Wendy.

One summer, I found adventure when a new family moved into town, and their youngest daughter became my best friend. She loved horses but didn't have one of her own, and I still had Franco. We would go riding together all the time and had the best of fun. We laughed and rode all over the county, down dusty country roads, across soft and pungent freshly disced fields, down the dry and sandy White Woman Creek, to the county fairgrounds, and anywhere else we could think of. We would ride all day, carrying sandwiches with us and knowing we had to have the horses back at the pens before evening chores to get a ride home.

When the summer ended and school started, riding had to shift to after school or on weekends. Still, riding with my best friend was what I lived for. I thought school was stupid and boring. I didn't really fit in with my classmates. I wore my cowgirl boots all the time, and no one was interested in horses like me. One boy who'd seemed my friend and played with me over the summer started the school year making fun of me.

I remember him making jokes about Franco and my cowgirl boots at recess. I don't know how my expression must have looked, but I remember telling him to take it back and feeling bonfire-heat in my face. He didn't, and I lost my temper and pulled a Franco, kicking him square between the legs with the toe of my boot! He dropped like a swatted fly and turned grey as he grabbed his crotch and began to moan and cry.

The shock and pain on his face told me I had made my point, and boy, howdy, did I feel vindicated. I'm not sure we ever really spoke again throughout our entire time together at school. That might not seem like a big deal to most, but my graduating class from high school only included twenty-eight students. Boy, did I ever set a boundary that lasted, well, a lifetime. I discovered in that moment that I could defend my horses. Unfortunately, I didn't yet know how to do that for myself, but somewhere deep down inside, a warrior was brewing.

When fall brought colder weather, my best friend and I rode only on nice weekends. She loved Franco like he was her own and wanted him so badly. One night, we struck a deal at a high school football game. I would not sell him to her, but if she completed my dare successfully, he would be hers for as long as they lived in town while remaining with me on my family's property.

The dare had to be worthy of the grand reward I'd offered, so we put our heads together and ultimately came up with the perfect scenario. She would cross a ceiling beam in the basketball gymnasium to earn Franco. The beams were easily accessible; you just had to climb the short concrete wall at the top of the bleachers to reach the bottom of the beams. The football team used the lockers in that gymnasium to change during football games, so the side door was unlocked. We formulated our plan and, during the third quarter, snuck away and into the gym. Up we went to the top of the bleachers and climbed the little wall, where we shook hands on our deal. Up onto the beams we then climbed, her for Franco and me as support and to prove my bravery. She started across slowly.

All was going well. We had, we thought, worked out the plan perfectly. We just failed to account for all the dust on the beam's bottom lip. With my stomach in knots and breath short I succumbed to my fear of slipping and falling about a quarter of the way across before deciding it was too slick and retreated. I was surprised that fear had stopped me, being the monkey I was in those days. My best friend, however, went all the way across! I don't know how she stayed focused and completed that dare. I climbed down to the court and slowly walked underneath her the rest of the way. My neck hurt from looking up and the exhale I released when she was back on the ground felt as though it had risen from the depths of my soul in relief. There was no way she was willing to fail.

I look back and think how crazy that stunt was and how lucky we were, truly lucky. It's a miracle she didn't slip and fall. We both had our guardian angels working overtime that night and sweating bullets. I cannot imagine the tanning our hides would have gotten if we'd been caught. Kids will do crazy things for a horse, and I honored our deal. Our friendship grew stronger after the dare, and we became inseparable. If I wasn't at her house, she was at mine, it felt as though we had been separated at birth.

My best friend moved away the following summer, which broke my heart. I remember crying for weeks. The pain and loss I felt was palpable. Everywhere in my body ached with the memory of her in my daily life. Grief and loss are real, no matter the age. To this day, I believe that no matter how young a person is, when they experience loss and a broken heart, they must be heard, their grief honored, and be given the time they need to process and heal.

Not one single person telling me it would get better, I'd make more friends, or we only knew each other a short time helped me feel better or heal quicker. My best friend's family had moved a few hours south, and my parents grew so concerned over my grief and despair that they took me down one weekend to visit. I guess it was a version of closure for me. I knew where she was and that she would be okay. But what helped me the most was the consistent soft, steady gait of my mare Wendy and my snuggles with Franco, my beloved horses, who were always there for me.

Wendy and her steady demeanor opened the door to new learning opportunities for me. I wanted to show horses just like the older girls, so, I joined 4-H, a youth development organization that supports young people in rural communities. I had to be age seven by January 1st to join, which didn't happen for me until I was sixteen days from my eighth birthday. I joined the program and chose a club and projects. Through that organization, I learned how to take care of horses and connected with local adults and parents who mentored as project leaders.

I loved every second of 4-H, soaking it up like a sponge. I could not wait until August and the county fair horse show. I went to project meetings with my horse, where we rode and practiced. They taught us what the judge looked for in each type of class, what each gait the horse did meant and felt or looked like, how to determine and ask for a proper canter lead, show ring etiquette, timed events, what was judged on the rider and the horse, so many things to learn, practice, and perfect.

Wendy and I went to every meeting and practice and did our very best. We worked hard all summer, and I continued to ride and practice every day. That first show was all try and plenty of fail for Wendy and me. I didn't win anything, and in the halter class, I couldn't even get my girl to trot when I needed her to. I felt disappointed and challenged. It was a moment that sparked an internal fire, a drive that brought determination to compete and became very familiar as I grew older.

After that first show, I spent my time watching the other horsemen and horsewomen who were winning, breaking down what each did successfully, and then figuring out how to mimic each movement they executed with my horse. There I would be watching, mimicking, and practicing in the grandstand. Those riders unknowingly taught me how to fail forward and how to train horses to win. With each attempt, I had to listen to the feedback Wendy gave me and adjust my communication to her needs. It was the only way to achieve my goals together with her and has become a lifelong practice for me in so many ways. By our second county fair horse show, we were proudly in the ribbons, and there was no stopping us or my determination.

At the same time I was learning to successfully compete in the show ring, I was experiencing a new threat in my neighborhood. After my sexual assault years earlier, I continued playing in the neighborhood with close friends I trusted. I was cautious with boys I didn't know but felt no need to be so toward the men welcomed by family and neighbors. A new single father had moved into my neighborhood with his kids, all of whom were quite a bit older than me. He seemed unassuming and friendly. I didn't feel afraid of him, and he was an active participant in the community. I did notice, however, that he always seemed to focus extra attention on me.

I did not know then to be afraid or cautious around

him, but looking back, I realize his behavior made me a bit uncomfortable. I could not seem to be invisible around or from him. In the culture of the early 1970s, it was normal and accepted when an adult male told a young girl that she looked pretty or that he liked her clothes or hair. No one thought twice about it and that made pedophiles able to hide in plain sight.

When no one else was around, he tried to hug and kiss me on the lips after complimenting me. I no longer felt safe and just wanted to run away. Hugs that were too long and included gentle strokes along my back which made my skin crawl. Breathing in my hair while lingering too long during a hug. Rubbing the small of my back too far down or touching my thigh. No one noticed.

"Shh, don't tell anyone. This is our secret" is never something a child should hear. *He* was supposed to be safe around. I was supposed to be safe in my own neighborhood. He was a parent and a trusted member of the community. I was a child in a small town under the age of ten, and no matter how fierce I felt, I was physically incapable of stopping a grown man from his behavior. Frankly, I never should have needed to stop him.

I felt small and weak; words like *No* or *Stop* would not form and come out of my mouth. I felt frozen inside with nausea driving vomit up my throat but never out of my body. I wanted to escape his eyes, his touch, his horrid smoker's breath, and the heat from his whispers in my ear. He was always around, it seemed, and no adult looked twice at him.

I avoided him as much as possible. But the secret-keeping and *or else* threats seeped deeper into my soul, and I carried those words instead of getting into trouble or disappointing my parents by speaking up. The grooming and threats worked. I tried to become a bit more invisible after that. I would walk as quietly as possible in the halls, practicing not being heard or seen. If I were invisible, I figured, these things couldn't happen to me anymore.

As an adult, I believe that I could not have been the only girl he touched or groomed or assaulted. The perpetrator is so seldom the man parents worry about and so often the neighbor they trust. Did people know and look away, or was he truly successful at hiding his horrific acts? A stealthy predator, he successfully navigated the shadows and infiltrated my nightmares. A man who helped further steal safety from my childhood in a small town. Someone else in my life who demonstrated dominance and domain over me and my body.

Outside in the wilds of western Kansas with my horses and dogs, being invisible didn't matter. They were my family, my herd, my pack, and they always had my back. Wendy and I would ride all over with my dogs always in tow. In the summer of 1976, a new dog would join the pack while we were visiting Garden City, Kansas. We lived about two hours from that city, the largest community in our region. *Large* meaning there was a Kmart and the other big-city shopping venues there.

In the summer of 1976, all kinds of celebrations took place in the United States, including a bicentennial wagon train that crossed the country following the old Santa Fe trails. One of the acts touring the country featured a forty-horse hitch, which appeared at Beef Empire Days in Garden City. Beef Empire Days, a weeklong celebration, represented everything agricultural with carnival rides, displays, a parade, a rodeo, and all things state-fair-like. It was amazing!

My folks took me to see the rodeo and the forty-horse hitch. When it was time, handlers drove the team into the rodeo arena and around the perimeter, maneuvering all forty horses together in a few patterns. It was incredible to see all those horses working together and the driver handling them all primarily with verbal commands. I had driven a single pony, and they were driving forty horses; I was in awe. It was on this day Geronimo the dog found us. He was kind of a beagle-looking mutt who'd been following me around all day, we immediately became two peas in a pod. I don't remember why or how it was decided he was a stray, but the drive home included his presence. From that day on Geronimo and I were inseparable.

He was the coolest dog and loved to climb up on the roof with me. I would lean a ladder against the side of the roof for him, and up he would go. Geronimo, my friends, and I would run all over that pirate ship roof! I cannot imagine what the neighbors thought, looking out to see a mish-mosh of kids with bandanas on their heads, an eye patch or two, wooden swords in hand, thundering across the roof yelling and jumping with a beagle in toe.

Whenever I rode out across the plains on Wendy, Geronimo tagged along. I began to notice how tired he would get during those all-day rides, so one day, I got off Wendy and led her down into a bar ditch on the side of the road. I picked up Geronimo and put him up on my saddle. He just sat there as Wendy grazed, not bothered in the least by a dog in the saddle. Up I went with Geronimo positioned behind the horn and in front of me crosswise, and off we rode. He would just sit there until he quit panting, and then he'd jump off again.

This went on for a short time, me getting off and lifting him up, until one day I decided to see if he would jump up partway and let me grab him. It took a few tries, some coaxing, and many failed attempts. Finally, I rode down into a bar ditch again after having him stay by the road, positioned above us. Once in position, I called him, and—success! He took a few strides and jumped! I grabbed his front legs, and up he climbed. We had figured out a system that worked. From that day on whenever Geronimo would tire, he'd jump up to me, and off we'd go. Wendy was such a good horse!

Wendy's steady demeanor indeed empowered me. She provided a stable platform and friend for me to test boundaries and experiment on. I decided at one point that I wanted to learn how to stand on her back while she galloped. We'd been to the circus, where I'd discovered a new world of horse riding and tricks. The thought of feeling the wind blowing against my body as I stood on her back, like surfing, only I would do it on land and on the back of my horse! And so it began.

First the idea and goal, and then the trial and error. I knew it wouldn't work bareback as I was worried my boots would hurt her back. So, it would have to be done in the saddle.

I began by figuring out how to kick out of my stirrups, swing my legs forward and then back for momentum, and then use that momentum to swing upward. It did not work. I finally tried simply monkeying up atop the saddle on my knees at a standstill and working on my balance—tricky but doable. Once I figured out how to pop up onto my knees at a walk, I sped her up. I finally got the hang of popping up from my knees with a little hop and push off by the swell of my saddle, then squatting on my feet at a lope and could stay in that position for extended periods. I had watched the jockeys at the track in Holy, Colorado and mimicked their posture. It was finally time to slowly stand, and success!

I practiced long and hard until I got the hang of it and could stand up on Wendy's back as we galloped across a field. That feeling of risk, challenge, and success at achieving my goal made my confidence soar, all because of my horse. I kept proving to myself that I could do anything I set my mind to. The shadows of trauma had shaded my youth, never knowing where true safety existed outside of my home. But in this moment a beam of sunlight broke through the dark and I felt as though I came alive, like the sun was burning from my heart outward, like every fiber of my being was smiling and cheering me on.

Success gave me hope because I controlled my mind and body. Wendy was truly the perfect horse teacher for me at this stage. Who knew that steady and stable was the key? She did, and her lessons have stayed with me as a mentor and teacher, along with her mothering energy and love. That experience was the epitome of learning to walk before you run, a literal example. Such confidence I derived from all her teaching.

I showed her into my preteens and reached the juncture most horse kids do when it's time to graduate to their next horse. Wendy moved on to be a solid mount, babysitter, and teacher for our neighbor's first granddaughter. There, Wendy was loved beyond reason by another smitten little girl. I believe every little girl needs a horse, and every horse deserves their very own little girl. Wendy's teachings have lasted a lifetime, and I am forever indebted to her.

CHIEF

I WAS AT THAT SPEED-JUNKY age that so many horse girls go through. I still wanted to run barrels. It was time for a new challenge on a new horse. Go fast as hell, turn, and burn. For that I'd need a barrel horse. We started our search and drove east in the frigid cold of winter to Hutchinson, Kansas, to see a red roan gelding that was an experienced barrel horse. His girl had gone off to college, and it was time for him to move on.

For me, it was love at first ride. He was good-looking, fun, and fast. The family selling him had other horses that piqued my never-ending curiosity, including a unique young stallion: a Russian Curly Bashkir horse they had won in a raffle. He was dun in color, and his hair coat was wavy, with a corkscrew mane and tail. I had never seen anything like him or heard of his breed. He had a lovely personality and good conformation. The family was standing him at stud.

Over the years, I've come across other curly crossbreed horses in the Kansas-centric region that I'm sure trace back to the genes of that imported stallion. You just never know what you might discover. That young stallion lit a little fire in my heart, that one day I might have my own stallion and that he too could be a polite gentleman. That spark would one day become a dream come true. Running across curly horses always takes me back.

The red roan gelding came home with us, and I named him Chief. He was so athletic and fast. I couldn't wait for spring to start training with him. He knew his job, though I was a beginner at competitive speed events. When the weather turned nice, I rode him like crazy and practiced constantly. We developed a quick partnership, but I soon discovered that with each practice session, he got a little hotter and soon began rearing at the gate before each run.

That first summer, I rode Chief all over the county with my best friend Shelly and her horse. Shelly had moved with her family to our community, and she was as horse crazy as me. We had the most important thing in common, our love of horses. She and I were a bit competitive—best friends everywhere except in the show ring. That's where the gloves came off!

I grew up in a small community, and back in those days, each county had a fairground. Ours was extensive: a full-size rodeo arena with bucking chutes, roping chutes, a grandstand, a refreshment stand, stock pens, etc. The county fair would include a horse show, a rodeo, livestock shows, 4-H project competitions, a carnival, a parade, and a dance. The fair would last nearly a week, and everyone in the county would show up. At least one other horse show would be hosted at those fairgrounds each summer, and we had access to the facilities year-round.

Like most kids in their preteen to early teens, I thought I knew everything about horses. I spent a long time watching others and experimenting until I figured it out for myself, because I didn't really know who or how to ask for help with training beyond our project leader's skills. Chief was fast and fun, except right before we would run an event. Didn't matter which speed event, he would get anxious and start rearing, and I do mean fully rearing.

The thing was, I wasn't afraid. I figured out how to sit forward when he went up. People would grow fearful when Chief initiated that behavior, so I agreed to try everything to solve the problem, including following unsolicited advice from everyone on the Little Britches Rodeo circuit. This youth rodeo program was offered to kids up to age nineteen, had junior and senior categories for boys and girls, and included speed events, rough stock riding, and even bull riding, and that was where I turned to compete.

My mom, who was not a horsewoman, drove us all over Kansas, Colorado, and Nebraska to Little Britches rodeos and 4-H horse shows. She was always supportive of my dreams and goals and learned to drive a truck and trailer just to take us to shows. I kept racing despite Chief's rearing problem. The following is all the advice I can remember on how to solve it: Face him away from the gate until it's time to run so he doesn't see what's going on, lope or trot him in circles on the outside without stopping until time to run, change bits, change to a hackamore, use a tie-down so he can't go up, and bust a bottle with warm liquid over his head when he goes up, so he thinks its blood running down his face to scare him into stopping the behavior.

One cowboy yanked me off at a rodeo and kicked Chief under the belly a bunch of times after he'd reared up. Such efforts went on for some time yet didn't stop the rearing. The truth was, I was young, inexperienced, ignorantly stubborn, and a kid. I suppose Chief and I had the "stubborn" part in common. I did not like how everyone was taking over my problem horse, especially the cowboy who yanked me off of Chief and proceeded to abuse my horse repeatedly. I felt guilt and remorse, even shame for not protecting Chief, but powerless to stop it. Fear was driving people's actions, as well as a prevalent belief in dominant training.

One of the great things about Chief was that he never hit a barrel. After our first season, we happened upon a rare occasion to run a full pattern for practice—no preparation, just a little warm-up, and then bam, run the barrel pattern. The idea was for him never to know when it was coming so he wouldn't get so anxious. We left the barrels up and just rode with them in the ring at all times so he wouldn't associate them with only racing. It was working beautifully.

One day I decided to just run a pattern. As we were making our first turn, I screwed up and pulled him into the barrel with his shoulder as we were coming out of the first turn. He was so surprised by hitting the barrel that he jumped sideways and forward hard. Suddenly I felt a shock of pain run through my nose, into my eyes and what seemed straight to the brain. My head snapped back and I grabbed for the saddle horn to stay atop my galloping horse.

I had been out over his neck to drive to the next barrel, and as he jumped up, I was hit in the nose by the top of his head. It broke my nose and hurt like hell, but I didn't come off, just held on in a daze as he finished the pattern. There was blood all over my shirt, saddle, and my horse by the end of the run. It was my first broken nose but not my last. However, I never broke it that way again! I learned two important things that day: My horse knew his job, so I needed to stay out of his way, and not to get so far up and over his neck that I could get my nose broken again. Pain can be a great teacher.

Donna Helmbold was a horsewoman and trainer in my hometown. She was married to a farrier, a giant of a man, and a gentle giant at that. In my eyes, they were the ultimate equine power couple. Donna modeled traits as a horsewoman that I still aspire to. She was a student of the horse, which I didn't truly understand until later in my life. She participated in all kinds of events with her horses, each of which was a world-class barrel horse. She is one of my heroes and part of the reason I wanted to run barrels.

Here's where Donna came into the picture. I got brave and reached out to her for help. This was a big deal for me, even at this age, as my trauma-driven, extreme independence was already playing a major role in my life.

She gladly offered advice and told me to seldom practice a full run. She also gave me a plethora of training exercise ideas to keep Chief in proper form without ruining him. I did what she said, and he got better. Chief and I qualified for the National Little Britches finals in Colorado Springs, Colorado, two years in a row, and I loved the experience of competing and making new friends from all around the country, but eventually, we both burned out.

I remember late one Sunday evening headed home from a rodeo. We stopped in Punkin Center, Colorado, at a small truck stop restaurant. Sitting at the table waiting on our food it took all I could do to fight to stay awake long enough to eat. My feet ached, and my back was so tight I wanted to cry but I couldn't muster the energy. I sat staring across the room at a young man who looked like I felt; he had dark, deep circles around his eyes, shoulders slumped, staring at the table with a zoned-outexpression on his face, mouth hanging open. After a moment, I realized my expression was the same, and so was my mouth. That was the moment I acknowledged I was done with rodeo as a competitor.

I soon became interested in traditional show classes again instead, and decided to turn Chief out for the winter. Once spring arrived, we started training for horsemanship, western pleasure, showmanship at halter, and even reining, but no speed events. When I took speed events off the table, we developed a deeper connection, and Chief blossomed.

At the same time, I was discovering boys and dating, or maybe the appropriate perspective is that they were discovering me. I wasn't comfortable alone with boys; I preferred group hangs. You see, one of the lessons I learned was that my body was attractive, and it seemed many of the males I was exposed to seemed to think that, when no one was around, they could attempt to help themselves to it.

I used to spend the night with some of my friends. One night at a girlfriend's house I was awoken by her older brother, who invited me to his room for a little fun. Wink, wink. His breath smelled of cigarette smoke and Marijuana. I had awoken to him whispering in my ear with a distinct intoxicated slur. He was caressing my arm through the covers in a fumbling gesture. I was startled and too afraid to respond at first. My heart felt as though it would beat out of my chest, my throat closed, and I began sweating profusely. My groggy sleepy body suddenly shifted into a freeze response. I felt like a deer in headlights anticipating the worst outcome. It felt like forever, but when I finally spoke, I said I will not go with you and threatened to wake up my friend, his sister. I was maybe twelve at the time.

I look back now and wonder where I got the courage and fortitude to respond that way, and I'm grateful I did. I suspect it had everything to do with the lessons the horses were teaching me. He wasn't the only young man to try to coerce me into his bed. It didn't feel good to be desired in this way. That night became another secret, buried away. What if his sister found out? Would I get blamed? The culture and messaging ate at me, and I protected those secrets and people from the light. I believed my shame and guilt, which told me it was my fault and that I would be blamed.

While I was dodging and dancing away from unwanted

male attention, I was also building confidence and skills with my horses. Chief was doing fantastically as a traditional show horse. We were winning. He was so athletic that I could get him to do all kinds of moves. That first summer of showing him in Western performance events, my family and I had gone to see the Royal Spanish Riding School riders and the royal Lipizzan horses in Garden City, Kansas. They were amazing! Some of the riders rode without stirrups, and they would longline the horses while performing airs above the ground. They demonstrated war maneuvers, during which the horses would leap into the air and kick out with their back feet. The Lipizzans would rear to a three-quarters position and hold themselves stationary. It was thrilling; my favorite were the dressage moves like the piaffe and passage, and I especially enjoyed it when the horses would canter in place.

After the show we went backstage to see the horses and meet the riders, I was giddy with excitement. It was heaven, and I wanted to ride like them. I decided that I wanted to go to the Spanish Riding School. The thought of sitting atop one of those magnificent white stallions and feeling the power of those movements made me vibrate with joy in every cell of my being. I just didn't know how that would work, since everyone enrolled were men. It was the first time I remember feeling like something was not possible because I was a girl.

I did, however, take a few dreams and ideas home, where I successfully experimented with Chief until I could get him to piaffe, passage, and canter almost completely in place! I found that when I collected him, lightened and activated my seat, and stretched upward, he would join me with his back rounded. Bam—all was possible. He was so willing to try new things with me. I had no idea at the time how challenging it was to train such movements. I was just having fun. Truly, I think I'm a better trainer and partner when I believe it's all just fun and games.

Chief was an amazing teacher and partner. He taught me some painful lessons and forgave all the abusive things I had done to him. I hadn't known the difference between dominance-based and consensual training and followed some counterproductive advice to solve problems that I'd created. Hindsight is 20/20. He offered me forgiveness, as I believe all my horses have done throughout my life.

He kept giving me more chances to do and be better. He held the heart of a girl who made mistakes and needed a horse to love and protect her heart and mind, if not her body. His willingness to forgive and be there with me on all those adventures gifted me with another layer of confidence and strength. He, along with my other horses and animals, was my sanctuary from unwanted attention. I didn't have to hide; I could be me, a horse-crazy girl safe with my four-leggeds.

Chief eventually moved on from my herd to a family in north-central Kansas. He hadn't run speed events in several years, but a trainer who'd moved to Colby was spectacular with speed horses and keeping them healthy and sane. We made the deal, and the following summer they started running him again competitively. They figured out the secret sauce for Chief's mental health and proceeded to break state records in barrels and poles while winning all manners of awards.

I believe in my heart that his break from running timed events mattered. Focusing on something other than games and speed helped him. I saw him a few years after we parted at an event. He was levelheaded, looked healthy, and was being loved on by one of his kids. His eyes were soft and gentle. I felt a warm tear roll down my cheek and my heart skipped a beat. My heart filled with love and a bit of sadness seeing him again. Chief had such an impact on my life giving me so many lessons. He would spend the rest of his days that way—being loved.

KINGBEE

THERE CAME A POINT WHERE I was ready to get serious about showing and competing. I wanted a competitive horse. A friend of the family knew of a quarter horse, a nice gelding, whose girl was in college. So, it was time for him to move on. He was my dream horse at that stage. We met, and he was perfect, but he came with a $2,000 price tag. Honestly, he was worth every penny, if not more, but that was expensive back in the day.

I didn't have the money, so I formulated a plan. I went to the local credit union and applied for a loan to purchase him. I asked my older brother Jerry to co-sign instead of my parents, a sign of extreme independence to come and got a job at the branch experiment station in our community. The position was full-time through the summer, which meant limited horse showing that year. The new horse, named KingBee, was also the reason I ended up selling Chief; I had to pay the loan. Grown-up decisions and sacrifices had to be made to achieve life goals. Letting go of one horse to move on to another came with some heartbreak, but I always believed each horse was moving on to a new life filled with love and purpose.

KingBee was a 16.2-hand high sorrel gelding bred on a quarter horse farm in south-central Kansas. The farm was famous for breeding big ranch horses that were levelheaded, athletic, and damn good-looking. Bee, as I nicknamed him, had won multiple titles with his previous owner. I believed him to be the next perfect teacher for me. He'd been sitting in a pasture a year or two while his previous girl was in college, so a tune-up and some relationship-building was needed. I purchased him as an investment in my goals and future and didn't plan on having a heart connection with him. I was young and naïve—I didn't realize at that age how important a role my heart played. Not that it mattered. I fell in love with him anyway.

You know, I had tried this tactic once before with my first pair of show lambs. I decided I would not get attached to them. I went so far as to only call them by their ear-tag numbers: Eleven and Twelve. I knew they'd be going to slaughter as a part of the project. The intent was to learn how to raise sheep for production from start to finish. Each lamb was judged on conformation, finish, and how the product—the meat—turned out, which was referred to as "how they would hang."

I handled those two lambs every day after bringing them home. They started off skittish and would run laps around their pen when I arrived to feed them. It didn't take long before they realized I delivered their meals. Food opened the door to curiosity and trust, along with my gentle demeanor and how I talked to them. My internal conflict, trying to compartmentalize my feelings for them, just wasn't working. Within days my heart lit up as they began to engage with me and allow me to start to touch them.

I trained them how to be shown in classes and how to stack, which meant standing in a defined posture while slightly pushing against my leg to show muscle definition. It didn't take long for me to fall in love with them. They had lovely personalities and would come to me whenever I appeared and called to them. I took them for walks and would talk to them. It felt like they were companions instead of eventual food. I experienced inner conflict around following through with my project or keeping them as pets.

We leased land two miles from our house next to a small community, next to a grain elevator on the outskirts of Horace, Kansas. We kept the horses, barns, and smaller livestock pens on the same pastures where we had milk goats and my two sheep. One summer day I went over to work with Eleven and Twelve in my little vehicle, a two-door box of a car with a small back seat. When I arrived, there were no sheep to be found.

I looked everywhere and called and called for them. I was in a panic by the time I had checked all the barns, pens, and pasture. was in a panic sweat, running about the property yelling; Eleven, Twelve, over and over. Suddenly, it struck me that they were gone, off the property. So, off I went in my little car with my Australian shepherd in the passenger seat. We drove the road next to the pasture and crossed the railroad tracks into Horace.

I drove slowly and methodically, treating the roads to and fro like a grid, looking up and down the streets and alleys and peering into backyards. I stopped often, asking folks out and about whether they'd seen my two lambs. Startled and confused gazes looked back, and folks would slowly and confusedly answer no. As we went along, finally, a few people mentioned having seen them and pointed me in the right direction. I finally exhaled, not realizing I had been holding my breath in a frantic state. As my shoulders began to lower, I felt a small sense of relief I was on the right track.

The sheep had gotten separated during their journey. I found Twelve first. I'd brought a can of grain with me, so he wasn't hard to catch. The thing I hadn't considered was how I was going to get them home. If you know anything about sheep, you know that if you sit them down like dogs, they'll stay. So, I sent my dog to the back seat, where he sat directly behind me. And then, with much effort and pushing from behind, I placed Twelve in the back seat opposite my dog as he leaned toward the window. I cranked up my little POS car with its twin-carb sewing machine-sounding engine, and we were off. On the hunt for lamb number two, all I could hear was a nervous dog panting, periodic bleats, and feel my blood pressure pounding in my head.

Off we went looking for Eleven, my Australian Shepherd looking side-eyed at Twelve and Twelve leering back cautiously, both unsure of the situation. It only took a few minutes driving to find Eleven. He was a bit tougher to catch, but the can of grain finally did the trick. Not thinking about my passengers, when I spotted him I quickly parked leaping from my car leaving the door wide open. I shifted to a panicked state of containment spotting the backyard gate open at the house he was grazing by. I speed walked toward him trying not to run and with only a few zags and some good luck chased him through the gate and into the yard. Once there, I shut the gate, went back to the car for the grain, and found the driver-side door wide open with both passengers still in place looking at me unsure of what to do.

I grabbed the grain and slammed the door as I ran back to the yard to catch Eleven. He was settled and grazing in the yard when I entered, I took a few deep breaths and very carefully approached as I shook the grain. He met me halfway and I quietly took hold of him. All of their handling for the show ring paid off. I picked up his front end placing his feet just inside the door and, Eleven jumped right in. With a bit of effort, I turned him and sat him down in the front passenger-side bucket seat next to me, and we headed through town. I cannot imagine what people thought as we drove down the street with me at the wheel, accompanied by two sheep and a dog looking out the windows.

By the time the fair rolled around, my heart was attached to Eleven and Twelve. I showed them both in market classes, and we placed at the top of our category. The last day of the fair came with a livestock sale, during which each of us sold our project animals at auction. People from our community would purchase them, sometimes giving them back to the kid, but most often they all shipped to slaughter. I had such mixed feelings going into the sale. I was proud of how well I'd done yet very sad over selling them.

The toughest part of that lesson was still to come. My father purchased one of my lambs. Now, you might think I was about to get him back, but no. Both lambs went to slaughter, and the one Dad purchased went into our freezer. He wanted me to fully understand the lesson of livestock production. It was my responsibility to provide the best care and quality of life for my lambs and then, when they went to slaughter, to be grateful for the financial income and sustenance they provided for our family. He wanted me to understand the life cycle from a true animal husbandry perspective.

I cried when Eleven and Twelve shipped. I had fulfilled every aspect of great animal husbandry because I cared for them with love in my heart. During the first meal at home, consuming my lamb was tough. I remember coming home from the pens after helping with evening chores. The ever-common question of what was for supper was answered with lamb, and my stomach turned, and tears stung my eyes. I went to wash up, but I really needed a few minutes to cry and steady my nerves.

I stood at the bathroom sink, water running to hide my crying, and gave myself a pep talk to get through that meal. After all, if I didn't eat the meal, I wasn't truly honoring the sacrifice. Whenever I stop to think about it, I still shed a few tears. But I learned to look at the responsibility of caring for livestock in a different light. If you remove your heart from the equation, you don't fully honor the animal or the sacrifice. I am grateful for such a hard lesson but value life and contribution more deeply when it comes to livestock.

So, my naïve attempt to simply invest in Bee and not become attached failed, unsurprisingly. It took a bit for us to figure one another out. He came with buttons already in place. I was so focused on playing and experimenting with feedback from my new horse that understanding his training didn't take long. He was a great horse in the show ring with one little flaw: He didn't have good lead changes. He would grow tense when we attempted a flying lead change. I came to learn from our friend who helped me find Bee that a trainer in Hutchinson had worked on his lead changes when he was three years old to the point of bloodying his sides with their spurs, and the facility they used in the winter for this training happened to be, unfortunately, the state fairgrounds arena.

Bloodying a horse's sides with spurs takes effort, serious effort, and repeated action over and over again to break the skin. This had been no mistake; it was intentional, dominant, and violent action to force this young horse, not yet physically or mentally ready, into performing an action for the show ring. A three-year-old horse is a big baby, not fully mature physically until six to seven years of age. Learning this news brought mixed emotions of seething anger and grief at such intentional abuse.

I participated in all the events required to get all-around titles at every show we enrolled in. I wanted to win the show, not just a class. I learned that summer the importance of being consistent and placed in the top three for each class, putting me in the running for the all-around title each show. Our weak spot was reining and our flying lead changes, but luckily, back then, we could do simple lead changes in the patterns.

Bee did great that first summer, and we qualified for the state show. I was so excited, and I carried the underdog banner on my shoulders. We didn't have money, a fancy show rig, or a trainer to tune my horse up before each class, unlike many of the successful youths I competed against. It was just me, my horse, and a lot of hard work. I was really proud of what we were accomplishing on our own. The feeling of being the underdog and winning is like no other I've experienced—a sort of pride mixed with an I-told-you-so feeling, and it came from hard work and passion.

During our first state horse show together, I learned a valuable lesson about a horse's memory. As you'll recall, I mentioned that the arena we competed in at state was the same one where Bee had been spurred bloody as a three-year-old in training. He would become so tense every time we entered that particular ring, he seemed like a completely different horse. I was angry after the first class but then realized that something was off for him. He wasn't just being uncooperative. Understanding the experience from this perspective (that of the victim) involves a different kind of knowing. After that first state show, I found out what had happened to KingBee in that arena as a young horse, and after that, it all made sense.

We placed in the top ten of several classes that year, but he just wasn't comfortable or himself in that environment. Every year, he and I returned to the state show, and every year, he grew a little less tense. I'm not sure of the difference between me and his previous owner or why he performed better for her in that space, my only thought being he was ridden with dominance and was likely performing out of fear. Luckily, all those lessons in husbandry, in caring for my animals and providing the best care possible, translated into me creating the best experience I could for KingBee at that facility. I, unlike some riders of the time, preferred my horses to have personality and freedom, to find partnership with my mount. It made all those lessons with the horses more powerful, and having been victimized and dominated, I continually sought ways to partner with my horses.

My goal and dream of "world dominance" in the show ring with Bee changed after his abuse came to light. It was a turning point for me, where partnership grew more important than winning at all costs. I had made a few mistakes that summer, one of which was to punish Bee after a bad reining pattern at a show. He didn't spin or pick up his leads quickly enough for me. So, I schooled the crap out of him, feeling frustrated with no trainer as a support system. My ego had been bruised, and I took it out on him. The shame and guilt I experienced after that inexcusable behavior forever changed me. How do you apologize to a horse? You do better, that's how. And so, I did.

Personal experience connected me to Bee's perspective even more during the summer I was fourteen. Our traumas stemmed from dominance and violence, and that summer, I discovered a different kind of sexual assault, date rape. I was interested in a college-age guy staying with his parents for the summer in my hometown. He and I would talk and flirt when we'd bump into each other. It was the first time I felt truly attracted to the opposite gender, I'm sure at that age I was driven by the awakening of my hormones.

One night, we went riding around in his truck, listening to the radio, holding hands, and flirting. We pulled over and started making out at the fairgrounds. He got a bit handsy and headed for third base. My heart started to pound. I was confused, attracted to him, and turned on while terrified at the same time. I suddenly didn't want to take things further and asked him to stop, but he just kept saying it would be fine and to relax. He kept referencing his needs as a man—and didn't I want to make him happy? I didn't want to be known as a tease, did I?

What I learned in that moment was that a freeze response is real. I said no several times and yet he didn't stop. I stopped responding and felt as though I was simply a doll he was maneuvering for his needs. He removed my jeans and underwear, and I was completely unresponsive. I felt as though I was in some other place, but I still felt what was occurring to my body. I was not taken into consideration at all, simply a toy for him to play with and be satisfied by.

I felt numb and then my mind went slightly elsewhere, his voice and grunting sounded somehow distant even though he was on top of me. I felt the distinct pain of his penetration and very quickly felt the shocks of electricity that come with little tears in the flesh and the sting of bleeding. I just wanted it to stop, but knew from experience it would not until he completed the act to his satisfaction. My body was simply a means to an end. When he was finished and I could get up, he simply told me to pull my pants on and he'd drive me home. I was in shock and pain.

Later I would learn the term "date rape." How could he not honor my request? How could he not recognize that my body was frozen and stiff? How could he not notice the tears running down my cheeks? How could he continue to violate me and live with himself? After he'd satisfied his needs, he drove me home and never spoke to or acknowledged me again. It was physically, psychologically, and emotionally painful and degrading. Once again, my body had become a source for a male's pleasure and dominance. I felt shame and guilt for not stopping him as if I could have. It was a breach of trust and something I came to expect from males. And so, I donned another layer of invisibility as I draped a mental cloth over another secret.

I tried over the last few years of high school to date. One classmate I went out with was a true gentleman while another was like constantly fighting off an octopus, even while we were at the movies!

The duality of my existence became challenging. I began focusing more time on my horses and my goals, one of which was to escape my hometown and never look back. KingBee helped me get a scholarship to Park College to ride for their equestrian teams. He went with me to school my freshman year, making that transition into college life and the beginning of adulthood safer because I had my best friend with me.

I can't talk about this period without mentioning the Seventh Cavalry. Somewhere around the age of fifteen or so, I met a group of cowboys from around Western Kansas who called themselves the Seventh Cavalry. They were all in their late teens to early twenties. I don't remember how we met, but I started dating one of the guys for a very short time. The guys ran around together in pickup trucks, going to rodeos and fairs, among other things. I didn't date the young man for long, but I stayed friends with most of them, and we would often hang out together.

Those guys would do all kinds of things like stop at friends' ranches and take turns jumping on random steers in the dark to see who could stay on the longest. It was always crazy stuff like that. We attended concerts as a group and went out dancing all over Western Kansas. The thing was, these guys were safe. The epitome of the word "gentlemen." Not once did they ever try anything with me. The Seventh Cavalry respected me as a human and a friend. It was one of the first times I felt seen by guys as a person instead of an object. I felt as though I was just one of the guys, except when they would open doors for me or be protective when we were out gallivanting around the country. They were welcome at my house anytime and would often just show up to hang out or chat whether I was there or not.

One of the guys and I were particularly close and at the

end of one summer he followed me back to school for my sophomore year of college. Jim was a tall, lanky cowboy, always in tall boots with his wranglers tucked into his boots, a button- down western shirt, a dew rag around his neck and a black cowboy hat that looked like it had been stomped by cattle and covered in sweat stains. He didn't dress like this for show, this truly represented who he was and how he lived his daily life on a ranch. He drove his pickup while I drove mine, pulling my trailer loaded with my horse behind me.

On the way to Kansas City, we stopped off at a McDonald's. When we were back on the road, he was ahead of me, and I remember watching him put shaving cream on his face and shave in his rearview mirror as we drove along the highway, using his coffee cup to dip and clean his razor. It made me laugh and smile. Jim was innovative, he found solutions in the most creative ways, just like most of the ranchers and farmers I knew. A kind of baling-wire-and-duct-tape-can-fix-anything mindset.

I moved into the women's dorms for that year at college, and Jim would sneak in after hours and sleep on my floor, since men weren't allowed in our rooms after 10 PM. I asked how long he planned to stay, to which he replied that it would be until he got bored or thrown out. I had introduced him around, and everybody in the dorm liked him. He was fun and funny and an all-around great guy. He went from room to room, crashing on different floors for nearly eight weeks. He stayed until he had to go home to the family ranch for the fall harvest. We had a great time!

Those guys opened a door I will always be grateful for. They saw me as a friend and treated me with respect, not a lesser gender. If it weren't for them, I may not have sought therapy and healing in college. I owe a big thanks to those cowboys in black hats, snot rags, and tall boots, the Seventh Cavalry. Thanks, fellas!

KingBee was also there when I acknowledged to myself a deeper truth: I liked girls. College was far enough away from home and small-town life that I was able to explore my sexuality. I always knew I didn't like guys as much as they did me, but I thought maybe it was because of my trauma. I knew they didn't smell good to me like something was off. The first time I kissed a girl, I had a light bulb moment, and everything made sense.

It was my freshman year when a group of us girls went to Ohio with a classmate; we'd decided to stay at her family home for spring break. We were all broke college students, and it was free room and board. We had fun there, often going to college parties with her older sister or just hanging out and laughing together. One of her friends from high school was hanging out with us and flirted with me when no one was paying attention. The attraction was mutual, and we began sneaking moments together. Glances that turned into our eyes meeting and connecting, held in one another's gaze. When she looked into my eyes my breath would catch, my heart would begin to pound, I would feel butterflies in my stomach, and it felt as though I was beginning to melt like butter as I came alive.

One night, we were all up late and hanging out in a bedroom, telling stories and laughing. Slowly, one by one, each person headed to bed until it was down to just three of us. Our friend climbed into her bed and eventually fell asleep, and that was when we started making out. I had never experienced an attraction like this with guys. My body felt magnetized to hers. Her lips touching mine lit me on fire. Her caressing touch felt like static electricity on my skin. I wanted to take her in with my eyes and savor every divine inch of her body. I wanted to taste her on my lips and breathe in her intoxicating scent. Everything about her I desired, and my body came to life in ways I never knew possible. One kiss led to another and so much more.

That was the first time I had sex with another woman. Suddenly, it all made sense to me, and I just knew what to do to please her. Every response her body gave me directed my every action. She told me what she needed and mod-eled consent and physical intimacy in a healthy way. My experience with her also freed me from the idea that I was irrevocably broken because I didn't want men. There were guys I found attractive but did not want to sleep with—not because there was something wrong with me, but because I was gay.

Not long after my spring break experience, I met my first serious girlfriend. She was a local where I went to college and kept her horse at the college barn. By the end of freshman year, we had taken things to the next level, and I was in love. We spent many hours on the phone that summer after I went home to western Kansas. My Seventh Cavalry cowboy friends didn't care that I was dating a woman, and in fact it happened around the same time my Seventh Cavalry buddy Jim went back to school with me.

My girlfriend and I were inseparable and on the down-low, because I had not publicly come out of the closet and didn't really think I needed to. I got a lesson in prejudice late that fall when I was outed by a classmate and her friends. They were so venomous and angry at my difference. I was ill-prepared

for this experience. I had never really fit in, but I also had never been attacked for being myself, at least not to my face. I had believed that they were my friends. We shared the love of horses, we were classmates, we went to horse shows together, and we had even hung out and had some laughs.

Oh, how quickly the tide can turn and how lethal and devastating words can be. I would like to say that I took it in stride and no one could knock me down. In truth, it hurt to be stabbed in the back by people I thought were friends. To have such intentionally slanderous and hurtful things said and gossiped about among peers intended to do harm. Make no mistake, their actions were intentional, pointed, and meant to cause harm. They did injure my heart and soul, I cried and felt emotional pain in a way I hadn't known, for simply falling in love. The duality of that window of time does not escape me.

Ironically, at least one of them came out of the closet a few years later. I guess the idea is that if you're pointing the finger at someone else, no one will catch you. The most disappointing part was that the director of the equine program participated in outing me and treated me differently from that point forward.

My college girlfriend and I were together off and on for seven or so years. We broke up a few times and broke one another's hearts a few times as well. We had ups and downs and devastated one another by screwing around while trying to grow up. However, we also loved one another deeply and were there for each other during some pretty big moments.

One such moment occurred over Christmas break during my sophomore year. I stayed at school to be with her over the holiday and to take care of KingBee. I was a broke college student and always looking for a quick buck, so when an opportunity presented itself through a maintenance guy near our age who was working at the college, I agreed. We knew the guy; he would let us all hang out at his house and drink while providing the alcohol. The job was trimming a tree for a local homeowner, and he needed a truck to haul off the wood. I had a pickup truck, time on my hands, and needed the fifty bucks he offered.

It was a beautiful winter day, sunny and warm for the beginning of January, the kind of perfect weather you just need to wear a few layers under a jacket for. We stopped at a fast-food joint for lunch and then headed over to the house. Our buddy used the homeowner's ladder and fully extended it to scale the tree. I offered to steady the ladder as he climbed and thus stood at the base of the ladder and grabbed hold.

When he was halfway up the ladder, it snapped in two. His weight caused the top half of the ladder to flip straight back, and before I knew what had happened, it struck me on the top of the head, knocking me unconscious—though from what I was later told by my girlfriend, my eyes stayed open the entire time. She said that the men were all running around, panicking, thinking I was dead. My girlfriend yelled for them to call 911. One minute I'd been lying there staring at nothing, and the next, very suddenly, I just sat up, scaring the crap out of them all. My girlfriend knew enough about first aid to drop to her knees behind me, wrap her arms around my torso to keep me still, and just hold me there while we waited for the ambulance.

I remember coming to and looking out past the trees and bushes at the edge of the yard. I felt like I was floating, and everything looked fuzzy or foggy. I could see the trees in the distance; one moment a blur of branches and limbs, the next all individual, shifting back and forth. I couldn't feel anything in my body, not numbness, I just felt as though I was tethered to my body and my eyes by a string of light and energy. I wasn't really there, but I was.

Blood had poured out of my nose as a result of the accident, but the impact didn't break the skin on top of my head. I kept touching my face just under my nose and feeling the sticky warm blood, moving my hands forward as though I was looking at it and repeating the phrase "I can't lose consciousness" over and over again. I do not remember seeing the blood, just feeling the sticky, warm moisture on my fingertips. I also remember feeling as though I might float away and that closing my eyes meant they might never reopen. Somewhere deep inside I knew things could come to an end that day and I wasn't ready to let go and slip away. I willed myself with every fiber of my being to stay awake and stay connected to myself and my body.

The ambulance arrived and off to the hospital I went. I distinctly remember the EMTs asking me who the president was and what a strange thing to remember. I thought it was a trick question because I couldn't recall whether Bill Clinton had taken office yet. My stomach was turning and the nausea would not subside. I was vomiting about every ten minutes by the time I was set on the table for X-rays. My lunch of a mushroom and Swiss burger left my body quickly and I have never had another one since. Eventually, I was sent home from the E.R. with a diagnosis of a severe concussion and a skull fracture and with oral medication for the pain. Oral medication for someone who could not stop vomiting. Really?

Back home with my girlfriend, I couldn't keep the meds down and just kept vomiting. The nausea was still ever present and my head was throbbing. My body hurt all over from the accident and the adrenaline. I couldn't stand light or sound; my eyes ached, and being spoken to rang in my head like striking a gong. Every time I violently threw up what was now blood and bile, it made my head hurt even worse, if that were possible. I just wanted the pain and the symptoms I was experiencing to stop for even a few seconds of relief.

That evening, my girlfriend took me back to the ER, and when I was finally seen several hours later, the young doctor gave me a shot to settle my stomach, which made me drowsy. The doctor told her my vomiting was being caused by the blood draining into my stomach instead of out of my nose and that, hopefully, it would stop. She drove me home, and within a short while, I felt relief; my stomach stopped churning and exhausted I fell asleep. She knew I wasn't supposed to sleep but couldn't get me to awaken, we were young and trusted the doctors, who just kept telling me to see my primary on Monday. She stayed awake, watching me sleep for the entire six or so hours that I was out, just watching my chest go up and down to make sure I didn't die.

When the medication wore off, I sat straight up and started projectile vomiting all the blood that had built up in my stomach. She called the ER, but they refused to see me. So, she called her primary as soon as they opened, who sent me straight to the hospital to be admitted. I was in the hospital for five days, and by the time my mom arrived from Western Kansas, they were concerned they'd need to drill a hole in my skull and put in a stint to relieve the pressure on my brain. Luckily the swelling came down before that was needed.

After my release from the hospital, I discovered I had a few deficits. I had a stutter, couldn't taste or smell, and was suffering from the worst headache imaginable. Moreover, my processing skills had been affected significantly. Anything said to me, I had to repeat to myself to comprehend the words. My friends would tease me about repeating everything. After all, it was how we had always engaged with one another. Constant teasing and bantering were my world with my friends. What they didn't know was that I was internalizing my frustration and shame. I wasn't the same quick-witted, sharp-tongued smartass they'd spoken to just a few weeks prior and I was devastated by my sudden deficits with no solutions or coping skills for this turn of events.

I was so frustrated with this complication that I began repeating everything in my head and stating out loud, "Hmm," to create enough of a pause to allow me to process what was said to me. Still, they teased. By the end of that spring semester, I was pretty tangled up in my own head. I cried a lot in private and remained incapable of communicating what I was feeling to my friends or family. My brain was broken and healing, but because I looked the same on the outside, with no long-term, visible scars, no one seemed to understand my altered new reality. I was broken, and my voice stolen in another way, in a literal way. Sexual trauma had stifled my voice in a way that created secrets, now my voice was stifled and stolen by a trauma that not only broke my body, but also broke my mind.

Despite the brain trauma and all my new deficits, one thing kept my drive alive. I wanted to ride KingBee! My horse and what he represented, along with holding my heart and confidence, kept me focused on getting better. I returned to him several weeks after the accident, against everyone's advice. When I close my eyes and reach back into that moment, I feel it all over again.

A beautiful winter's day, with sunshine warm on my face and the still-crisp air biting ever so slightly at my lungs. Hearing Bee's soft nicker as I entered the student barn warming my soul and providing a welcome respite from words. Feeling his coat and mane against my cheek as I hugged him for God knows how long, feeling loved and held in return, tears streaming down my face. He welcomed me like an old friend missing their soulmate or twin flame. Our hearts connected and intertwined. I had to have help saddling and bridling him, and used a mounting block to climb aboard. My girlfriend was there, supporting me physically and emotionally through the entire experience. She knew what it meant to me.

The sun felt so fantastic on my face as we rode to the cliffs overlooking the river. We just walked. I can still hear the gentle squeaks of my saddle, feel the soft rocking in my seat, and hear the crunching of the leaves under Bee's feet as he clip-clopped along. I can also feel the constant throbbing in my head, my squinting, feeling like every ounce of my body hurt. That short ride on my KingBee was everything I needed in that moment. He gave me hope that I could return to myself, could heal, could become what I dreamed of: a horse trainer and coach. I knew in the back of my mind that it would be a long, hard road, but in the saddle on that magnificent gelding, my Bee, I felt hope.

It took eleven months for that headache to subside. That summer after my accident my girlfriend and I moved to Western Kansas so I could take a year off from university to heal. I needed things to slow down and to be in a familiar environment close to family. My folks had moved that spring, and we decided to relocate to my hometown for the summer to help get my childhood home ready to sell.

That summer I also kept running into the man who had tried numerous times to kiss and grope me as a child when I had still been riding Wendy. I realized that my therapy was helping me, because my trigger, or activated energy, didn't feel overwhelming when I'd see him. All summer I revisited my experiences with him and felt an urgent need to take back my power and control. Honestly, I didn't know what that meant until one night late in the summer. We were at a large party, and he was there, joking and laughing.

In that moment I made a decision. I was going to seduce him and take back my power, reclaim domain over my body. My girlfriend knew who he was and what had happened and supported my decision, though I'm sure, reluctantly. So, I got tipsy and flirted with him. I became emboldened with my plan and as the night went on began to escalate from flirting to seducing. It wasn't long before he asked me to go home with him, and I did.

I remember him trying to kiss me and recognized his distinct musty and cigarette smoke scent from childhood. Moments came with flashbacks from my childhood, but I kept going determined to reclaim domain over myself with this man. We undressed, with my stomach turning in circles and my heart pounding, and when he tried to speed things along, I somehow had the fortitude to take control. I insisted he focus on foreplay and go down on me, all the while feeling the room spin slightly as I built my courage and confidence to keep going. Focused on being heard, I gave instruction on his every move, not for pleasure, ultimately for control. He wanted to penetrate me without protection, and I insisted on him using a condom. I allowed him to penetrate me on my terms ever in control. I was not turned on physically, emotionally or spiritually, there was no connection with this man other than repulsion for what he had done to me as a child.

And in that moment, I felt vindicated somehow. I told him to get off me, got dressed, left, and never looked back. I was nauseous and wanted to throw up from the experience, and yet I felt empowered at the same time. I took control, I didn't freeze up and shift into a victim state. I stood in my choices and enforced my boundaries with him. Some might think this a twisted gesture or uncommon, but it is not. I would never recommend this action to anyone else. But taking back control of my body in that environment with this man was a key component in my healing journey.

The loss of power or domain over my body had haunted me for years. Being in control has been a mainstay in my life. I do not like the feeling of being out of control; I don't get drunk, I don't do drugs, I have worked out religiously for long periods in my life, and I've controlled food, sometimes obsessively. Self-control can be a strength overused at times, but this moment with him was another step in regaining my domain over my experiences.

That fall I chose to attend a junior college close to my folks' new place instead of returning to my university to complete my four-year program. I needed time to heal from the skull fracture. What I didn't fully realize at the time was that my life would never be the same. That moment of impact from the ladder had changed me. I took classes that would transfer over so I wouldn't fall too far behind and allowed myself the space to heal.

In a history class I took at the junior college, I had to give a final presentation to the class. The presentation required that I speak publicly, and I was terrified. Cathy before the accident had spent countless hours preparing for and pre-senting public speeches. Through 4-H, I gave presentations up to the state level and to large audiences. Cathy after the accident was a different experience. My stutter, delayed processing, and speech issues were overwhelming and debilitating.

I remember sitting in class, waiting my turn. I could hear my heart pounding in my ears, I felt lightheaded, my palms were sweaty, my ears were ringing, and I couldn't focus. I swear I could hear the silent digital clock ticking ever so slowly. When my turn came, I stood, walked to the front of the class, and just looked out at everyone with tears running down my face.

I couldn't believe this was happening to me. I do not remember a word I said for my presentation, just that I raced through the experience as quickly as possible and then ran out of the classroom in a full-blown panic attack.

I couldn't breathe, my chest felt tight and painful, my head was pounding and spinning, and it felt as though my physical body was awakening from falling asleep all atingle. After that, I realized how things had changed for me. It was a moment where I wanted to be invisible, a familiar feeling that I hadn't felt much throughout college, but there it was, nonetheless. That moment of devastating epiphany back then took decades to overcome.

The summer after my sophomore year, Bee and I parted ways. My friend who had arranged the purchase of Chief by his next family called, looking for the perfect show gelding for a family he worked with. They had three daughters and wanted a dream horse for their girls. He had thought of Bee, knowing I was in college. I thought long and hard, and through much crying, decided it was time for Bee to have a next chapter too.

I had so much love for this horse who had been there and supported me through so many significant life changes. He was the first horse I rode after my traumatic brain injury; he helped me succeed in the show ring and get a scholarship to college, he taught me lessons of empathy and understanding and he had been my rock. I knew I was headed in a new direction soon to become a professional with less time for him. In my heart I knew he deserved more and so I chose to break off a small piece of my heart and let him go, to move on to his next chapter.

The family bought him, and those girls adored him. They showed him in 4-H and trail-rode him. He raised all three girls, and they were his last home. He's buried on their farm. I owe him so much for all my lessons, for the success and achievements he helped me acquire, and for the direction I chose in life. He, like those lambs Eleven and Twelve, opened my heart and he held it when I needed it protected and cared for. Thank you, Bee. I will always be grateful to you.

THE DIAMOND B RANCH

AFTER A YEAR OF RECOVERY from my TBI, I returned to college to finish my degree in equine studies. I had several horses that returned to school with me, whom I sold, one by one, to good homes and loving next chapters. I was preparing for a career in the horse industry and realized I couldn't work at a ranch and drag my horses along at the same time.

Near the end of my junior year of college, in need of a summer apprenticeship, I spoke to one of my instructors who suggested I call Jack Brainard, a world-renowned quarter horse trainer in Texas who produced top reining futurity horses. When it came to horses and my career, I had reclaimed my confidence and drive and didn't worry much about my stutter, so I picked up the phone and called. By the end of that relatively short call, I had my apprenticeship. My fear and anxiety turned from tension into excitement vibrating throughout my body. I was going to work for and learn from one of the best teachers and trainers in the world!

I packed up and headed to Texas with a suitcase and a saddle. The ranch had a young man learning to start colts, so each apprentice, including myself, and assistant trainers took over a horse who was around fifteen or so training rides into their start under saddle. That summer, I had twelve to fifteen horses to ride a day. The job came with new lessons and several occasions of being told after the fact what our colts didn't know—education by fire.

One of my first experiences at the ranch was with a young mare I brought in to saddle on my first day. I gently caught her and gave her a bit of a rub all over before heading to the saddling area. I quietly led her into position and as we arrived gently tied her habitually to saddle. The instant she felt the hard tie with no give, she sat back hard, snapping a line and sitting herself down like a dog with a start. Her actions jumped my heart into my throat and a dump of adrenaline that felt like twelve consumed espressos.

The result of my actions came with a scolding by a young assistant trainer. The mare didn't know how to tie, I was told after the fact, so why did I tie her? There was definitely a little *you dumbass* mixed into her tone. The lesson in that moment was profound: Never assume anything and ask all the questions. So, that's what I did, I'm sure, at times, to the great annoyance of others, but I was not going to make another mistake like that again.

The Diamond B was a ranch forged through hard work. We as trainers not only worked our horses, we fed, cleaned stalls two to three times a day, and turned our string of training horses in and out on rotations. We had Sunday off around chores, which meant that was laundry day. I didn't know it was possible to work as hard as we did and love it at the same time. It was not uncommon to return to our housing at the end of the day, shower, and fall asleep attempting to eat dinner. It was the kind of tired I felt in my bones, with a profound level of peace that resonated in the deepest caverns in my soul.

Jack was not only a great trainer and still riding at seventy-two years old when I went to work for him, he was also a great teacher. His approach to mentoring us resonated with me on every level. I also really appreciated that he preferred to hire girls. He said that women worked harder and trained better, and he valued our approach. It was the first time I was ever acknowledged professionally in a positive way for having a more feminine approach.

Jack was an interesting guy, well-read with diverse interests. Everyday mid-afternoon, we would take a watermelon break. Jack would go to town for coffee and come back with fresh watermelons, he loved watermelon, and we would gather around a picnic table as he cut up watermelon and passed it out. We would laugh and chat about our day and how our horses were coming along, and Jack would usually tell a story that would have us all belly-laughing on our way to our next colt. At the time I didn't realize he was teaching us how to build relationships and improve rapport and communication, just by sitting and sharing watermelon.

The training lessons I learned that summer are still foundational in my approach to training horses today. Every horse at that barn had a unique personality, and I learned to adapt my communication to their needs quickly. Each horse, however, needed the same foundational skill set to advance in their training; I just had to learn to adapt to each individual horse's needs to make that happen. I kept a daily training journal that summer that I still turn to today. Jack was always there to not only answer questions, but also to model what he was teaching. That first professional experience with Jack set up my expectations of an employer and as a leader. Leading by example has been a mainstay approach in my life thanks to Jack Brainard, which includes transparency not only about my success, but also my failures.

One horse I rode that summer, named Agent, was a light-colored chestnut gelding and petite in his build, but he was smart and athletic. I put my very first slide on that little horse, and I'll never forget that moment or feeling. Just me and Agent working in the big arena, loping circles. I set him up between my reins and asked him to soften in my hands, without overthinking I gently swung my feet forward as I rolled my back, exhaled, and said, "Whoa." He just sat down, slid two to three feet, and relaxed into a stop.

Everything felt easy in the moment, second nature, and a partnership like seasoned dancers on the dance floor. Moments like this can seem fleeting in my daily life with such a busy brain, but these simple moments are like two puzzle pieces fitting together flawlessly and settling in to home. That sliding stop did not come with excited vibrations; it came with a calm authentic resonance of a shared experience and a soft and gentle sigh at the end. I still strive for that level of connection and communication today. Fleeting moments of kismet and a gentle kiss of fate.

Agent also taught me how smart and determined he could be. The indoor arena at the Diamond B Ranch was at the end of the stall aisles. There were four rows of stalls with two entrances into the arena. We never closed the entrances off, not even to the outside of the arena. Jack believed our horses needed to learn to adapt to the environment and stay between our hands and legs, and so did we.

Well, one day, Agent caught me off guard by bolting down an aisle as we were loping past the entrance. I was not prepared, caught off guard, and about ate some dirt face first. I luckily reclaimed my balance in mid-shift of direction and stayed aboard, very startled and unsure of what was occurring. He shot into a stall with an open door with me on top and leaned into a wall, pinning my right leg and not moving. I was dumbfounded at his action and unsure of what to do. I didn't feel panic, just shocked and concerned about what just happened. Oh, and some pain since my leg was pinned with him leaning hard on it into the wall. Eventually, I got him off my leg and decided to dismount for safety reasons, then led him back into the arena. On I climbed after catching my breath to regroup, and off we went.

We loped at the far end of the arena, and he seemed fine. We then gradually worked our way back toward the aisles loping circles with no problems, until we went back on the track and tried to lope past the entrance. A quick dart at the last minute, and down the aisle we went again and into a stall. Evasion number two got Jack's attention, and he decided to enhance the lesson as we problem solved. Jack had the other trainers dismount, close all the stall doors, and sit remounted in the middle of the arena while he instructed me and Agent. I definitely felt the spotlight, but just didn't have time to worry about it.

Off we went while following instructions at the end of the arena furthest from the aisles, loping little circles and then spiraling out in each direction, finally working our way back toward the aisle entrances, still loping circles and getting closer and closer. Agent was doing fine staying between my hands and legs with his ears soft and listening, until we attempted to lope past the opening at the aisle. At the last second as were about to go by, he dropped his shoulder, and down the aisle we went. He couldn't find an open stall and eventually stopped at the other end of the stalls near the offices.

I couldn't get him to ride back down the aisle to the arena, so I finally got off and led him back to where we started. Everyone was told to dismount except me, and I took a deep breath and remounted. Agent and I were both breathing heavily and sweating profusely at this point. I wasn't sure I had the strength to keep going, but I gave myself a little pep talk and off we went. The other trainers were positioned on either side of the aisle gates per Jack's instruction.

The intention was for them to holler and wave at us to discourage his escape as we approached and then hopefully ride by without escape. I deepened my seat, expecting a lively ride, and we began the process again away from the aisles, starting with small circles at a lope and building outward. When we finally passed the entrances, they hollered and waved, and we went past the first time. But, the second time around, it didn't matter to Agent what the other trainers were doing. *Boom.* Down that aisle we went again with Agent in control and me along for the ride out of breath, tired, and frustrated.

Jack decided to take things up a notch and had one of the trainers get a broom, the flat, witchy kind, and wait by the gate with instructions to swing the flat side at us and make contact if Agent tried to escape again. Holy shit! I didn't know my seat could get any deeper in the saddle, but it did. Off we went to start the process over, loping small circles at the far end, then spiraling out into big circles, stopping and then rolling back to go in the other direction. I was talking to Agent the entire time telling him we just needed to ride by each time without escape. I was whispering a prayer to the universe and the horse ancestors to help end this evasion.

I was really concerned what would happen if Agent got hit with the broom. Would he get hurt or be blinded in an eye by mistake? Would he fall down with me or escalate and run hard into a wall? Would this ever come to a resolution and end? I prayed to everyone I could think of out of fear and hope, but kept going as instructed because that's what was expected of me as a professional. Besides, who was I to question this man, my employer, and mentor.

We built on the repeating lesson and worked our way down to the aisle end once again from the far end of the arena. We successfully loped by the entrance twice that time before he tried the escape, and this time just before getting to the gate, Jack yelled now and out from behind the wall came a broom. Thwap! It took Agent a minute to stop, and his momentum carried us hard into the broom, which made contact on the side of his head and neck. He stopped dead in his tracks and stood there blowing, both of us vibrating with shock and panting. I finally asked him to turn and go back into the arena, and after a little encouragement, he walked right off. We tested the theory with everyone in place about ten times past the aisles, and not once did he try and duck out again. Problem solved, albeit a tough day at the office to say the least.

Today I would explore physical pain or even mental fatigue as potential causal factors for his behavior, but I wasn't experienced enough to consider those options back then. Jack had the outside perspective and decades of experience to back up his decisions, not to mention it was his barn and his horse, and it worked. I learned a lesson in perseverance that day, along with the value and necessity of having a really great mentor and teacher who liked and respected horses. Jack valued the learning process for both rider and horse, and I believe he truly enjoyed teaching both horse and rider, a rarity in the industry. Agent never tried that trick again, diand I guess I'll never truly know what triggered his behavior that day. But I did learn that sometimes you just have to ride it out, in the saddle and in life with courage and perseverance.

My summer in Texas changed me for the better. I matured as a person and a student, and I left with a job offer after graduating from college. I returned to Texas to the Diamond B less than a year later with my B.A. in Equine Studies and went to work full-time. My first girlfriend and I were still together, but she relocated to Tennessee for school to become a dog groomer while I headed to Texas. The plan was for her to come to Texas, which never happened.

I discovered how much I really loved working with people and teaching with horses because I came to miss that component in my life at the Diamond B. The environment was stable, predictable. At the Diamond B, I always saw the same few people day in and day out. When it was an apprenticeship there was an end in sight and frankly it felt different. The idea of my reality as a trainer there just didn't fit my dreams and I was surprised by that discovery.

I was not open about my sexuality with my coworkers at the ranch, choosing to keep my personal life to myself. I had learned after being outed in college how mean and spiteful people could be, and I was afraid of the negative consequences that might occur if anyone found out. Unfortunately, I also discovered how prejudice could creep into daily conversations and how people tended to assume that others thought the same way they did. I happened into a work conversation about some barrel racing clients who were likely gay and heard some unpleasant comments regarding their sexuality, not because they were bad people or bad clients but because it was presumed they were gay.

In that moment, I felt smaller inside and responded by adding another layer of invisibility. I was right in hiding my true self from them and disappointed in who I believed they truly were.

My immaturity and trauma response guided my thought process; that, coupled with the blatant prejudice there, drove me to eventually leave the Diamond B Ranch. I decided to go back to Kansas City and into business for myself while also attempting to save my volatile relationship yet again. Sadly, it wasn't salvageable and shortly thereafter came to an ugly end. However, going into my own horse training business began a new chapter of growth, learning, and community for me.

My passion for teaching people and horses allowed my light to shine more brightly. I felt alive inside and excited for my future again, a future I was choosing. It took no time to grow my business, and I savored every moment of connection and growth. I stepped into my calling and out of any preconceived glory I had associated with training reining horses. It was so important for me to take that job with Jack to discover my own truth. Sometimes our greatest lessons are what we're not meant to do, experiencing what doesn't resonate. That discovery opened a door to a completely different life than I had planned, but this time it was based on actual knowledge and experience instead of a preconceived idea and fantasy.

SCARLET AND TATE

IT WAS WINTER WHEN I moved back to Kansas City from Jack's. My girlfriend and I found a little house in a rough neighborhood to rent. I went to work as a night auditor at a hotel and during the day sought opportunities at barns in the region to start training again. After a few months, an opportunity fell into my lap: a barn that needed a new manager and was experiencing financial hardship made me an offer. I jumped at the chance to get back in the saddle full-time.

The barn owners were inexperienced and had no idea how to run a boarding business and were new to horses and the industry. They thought we have horses now so let's buy a barn and board horses to offset our expense. An all-too-common occurrence, but one that has gotten me paid numerous times. The boarders at the said facility were also being terrorized by one of their own, a bully. This was my first foray into boarding facility management.

The barn was outside of Leavenworth, Kansas, and many clients were military families. The bully was a colonel's wife who liked to throw her husband's rank around. I stepped into the managerial role, evaluated the entire situation, and trusted my gut. Within forty-eight hours of starting the position, I had politely evicted the colonel's wife and her horses, met with all other boarders to provide them with the new rules, and began building my training and lesson program. I discovered my forte for management and good communication practices. It was an exciting discovery, especially considering that only a few years had passed since my skull fracture and subsequent mental deficits. But when it came to horses, I still had my ever-present confidence and faith in myself.

The boarders were now happy, and the facility was full. It took no time at all for my training and lesson program to fill. I was thriving professionally with a work effort and focus I had honed working for Jack in Texas. However, my personal life was a different story. My relationship ended in an ugly fashion a few months after I took over the barn. The pain and hurt we caused each other would not fully heal for several decades.

In the meantime, I developed friends and wonderful new clients. One of those clients bred quarter horses, and we worked out a deal. I would start under saddle and train her many horses. In exchange, I could pick two of her registered horses to keep as partial payment, with the rest to be paid monthly. I evaluated the herd and their bloodlines and chose a gorgeous three-year-old palomino gelding and his half-sister, a four-year-old, blood-red sorrel mare named Scarlet. Both needed to be started under saddle, and by summer, they both rode out beautifully. The lessons I had learned in Texas paid off and my training skills had advanced what seemed light years. All that learning and training down south seemed to come to me second nature now, like driving a car. I was thriving in my new role and savoring the diversity.

I was at the Leavenworth property for around two years when the owners skipped town and emptied their business accounts, leaving everyone high and dry. There were warning signs of financial issues and problems to come. They purchased a "vacation home" in Florida and had their personal horses sent down for the winter, never to return. When I had asked questions, I was always reassured all was fine and the company was doing great.

Suddenly, I found myself needing to move, find a different barn, and start over in less than thirty days. I even had to sell one of my horses. My gut had warned me, but I kept talking myself out of concern. I had an uneasy feeling about things but chose to bury my head in the sand, because I was thriving. I didn't want to sell either horse, but decided to put both up for sale and keep the one that didn't sell. I had been caught off guard, my own fault, and had to make some hard adult decisions. The Palomino gelding sold in a few days, not surprisingly. He was gorgeous in color, built beautifully, quiet, and rode like a dream. I loved them both dearly. They were polar opposites, and I didn't want to let go of either, but I followed through on the sale to get on with life. So, I kept Scarlet and that turned out to be one of the greatest gifts possible from the universe.

Scarlet was built to be a reining horse anatomically. Her sliding stops kept getting longer, and her spins were fast and hard. She had it all except good flying lead changes. I thought we'd do great on the show circuit, and I was right, but it wasn't in reining.

When I left my girl alone and let her choose how she wanted to ride, she would collect herself and jog-trot all day long. She always chose to travel like the perfect Western pleasure horse. I was not excited about the idea of showing Western pleasure on the AQHA circuit; I found it boring and everyone was doing it. I had loved the run and gun that came with reining horses, a consistent pattern since childhood, savoring fast and furious. But Scarlet was happiest being ridden in that way, like a western pleasure horse. I fought the idea for months, focusing on reining skills and rewarding her with her preferred way of going after each training session. What I learned from her over time was that we do our best and are our happiest when we get to follow our own unique path. Just like I had gifted myself leaving Texas for my own path and business.

Scarlet did not fit the ideal Western pleasure horse image; she was small compared to the other horses in that event, but that mare would turn on when we entered the ring, and she was flawless in her gaits naturally. She placed consistently in the top five at every show we competed in. She thrived and taught me to listen to the horse, not decide his or her future based on registration papers and breeding. Every horse I've owned since has chosen their job or at least a version of their preference. When I took her to shows I never had to worry or school her before a class. She would sit quietly and even often looked nonchalant, standing in the warmup pen, eyes half closed and back leg gently cocked.

At first glance a simple little horse outshone by all the glitz and glamour around her, but once we entered that ring she lit up and went to work. Suddenly, she was Marilyn Monroe, and all eyes were on us, flawless. She shined in that arena and in turn so did I. I was the professional putting in the work and winning in the ring. I had come a long way since 4-H shows being the underdog flag bearer. Scarlet taught me how to be settled and confident in myself by owning her skills and shining when the spotlight turned to her. No need to try and stand out, because who she was naturally did all the sparkling without pretense. I was so proud to be her partner and show her in Western Pleasure classes, because she was happy and joyful with her job.

I decided to breed Scarlet to one of Jack's stallions a few years after acquiring her. I prayed to the universe for a colt who would become my first breeding stallion. When she foaled, she had a gorgeous sorrel colt, whom I named Tate.

At two weeks old Tate had an accident while playing in turnout. He slipped in a bit of mud next to a metal door where the corner had been exposed and cut himself nearly to the bone on his front left fetlock. I was devastated knowing the likely outcome of his injury would mean he would never be sound or fulfill my dream of having him as my first stallion. I called my veterinarian, who came by, stitched up three separate layers of tissue, and cast his front leg. We crossed our fingers, said our prayers, and hoped he would heal and be rideable and sound. Every two weeks we changed the cast because of his fast growth, but that cast didn't slow him down one bit. He had other plans for his life that didn't include my worst nightmare. I would soon learn there was no quit in this horse.

Tate had the best sense of humor; he was funny and reminded me of Dennis the Menace. About four weeks into his wearing a cast I pulled up at the barn and found everyone peaking around a corner, laughing hysterically. When I got out of my truck, they waved me over, giggling and pointing. I looked around the corner, and there was Tate with his cast resting on top of the plastic bottom rail of the fence, just staring at it. All of a sudden, he lifted his cast and, bang, slammed it down on the rail. This action caused his cast to bounce and vibrate, and his little face lit up, his head bouncing along with the cast's vibrations. He repeated the behavior over and over, and we kept on laughing. Anyone who has worn a cast knows how itchy and uncomfortable they can be.

Little Tate cleverly found the perfect solution for his discomfort and entertainment. A problem solver of the highest accord, and eventually he would turn those powers toward his own entertainment and wicked trickery. I had discovered how funny and clever my boy was going to be. That laughter and joy he displayed would last a lifetime and enhance many lives with joy and hope.

When that cast came off, he was sound! I was so relieved and excited for his future. I began dreaming again about our what-ifs together and breathed a sigh of relief, embracing hope again at achieving my dreams with him. He never slowed down after that. He would lope circles around his mom in the stall, working his shadow like a little cutting horse. Round and round he'd go before suddenly sliding to a stop, facing the shadow on the wall, cutting it a few times back and forth, and then taking off like a shot in the other direction around her.

Scarlet was not thrilled and did not enjoy being a mother, much to my dismay. When Tate's testicles dropped, I had a glimpse of who he would be as a stallion, and his change in behavior displayed the kind of arrogant and defiant stallion I never wanted to handle, ride or breed. That discovery sealed the deal and I was so disappointed. My hopes and dreams for my own stallion were shattered not long after they had been dashed and reawakened. Those few months were quite the roller coaster ride emotionally and really tough to go through. I was disheartened and sad. He was gelded and became a wonderfully sensitive riding horse with a penchant for the girls, even as a gelding. I was disappointed that he wouldn't become my dream stallion, but I made the right choice. I have seen way too many horses become breeders that were not suitable for riding only to pass on those traits and produce unsuitable offspring.

The lessons in animal husbandry I learned as a youth also included responsible breeding practices. Those lessons easily carried forward to my decision-making about Tate, and later into many other breeding decisions with horses. I have always taken the responsibility of breeding and bringing new life into the world seriously. There had to be a plan and reason to breed each horse with a gameplan for their life, which can easily last 35 years. My lessons with a killer buyer and his wife, seeing all those unwanted and disregarded horses sent to slaughter without a thought for their future, stayed with me. If breeding operations and backyard breeders had these same lessons, maybe we wouldn't overbreed or breed horses with bad genetics and traits just to get a baby to play with.

After my breakup with my first serious girlfriend, my friendship with one of my female boarders, Sara, deepened. We began spending more social time together, and things eventually became intimate. She was the polar opposite of my first girlfriend in every way. I was her first female partner, first love, first lover, first cohabitation, first everything.

She had been there for me during my breakup. She cheered me on as a professional and truly believed in me. She was falling in love while I was climbing out of heartbreak and into healing. Looking back, I can recognize where I was emotionally and that I swung the pendulum to the opposite end of the girlfriend spectrum. I cared for her, but we were not a good fit long term. Her pursuit of me was like salve on a wound on my broken heart. They say the best way to get over someone is to get under someone else. I don't think that is actually true, it just distracts from the pain and life changes. The pain and lessons come back around eventually to be dealt with. But in the beginning my ego sure enjoyed being stroked, supported, and wooed.

Sara was very much in the closet, especially with her parents. This complicated things as I was very out of the closet now, and her mom did not like us spending time together which she vehemently stated frequently. We were both in our early twenties, and Sara had moved back home after college to get financially stable and get her own place. Watching her discover herself and explore her sexuality was fun for me, but I was much further down that road. It was invigorating helping her discover her body and sexuality.

I was bolstered by her immersion into our intimate life and joy discovering her true feelings. I loved providing a loving and supportive safe space for her awakening. It felt gratifying and loving to be that for her. We were together for several years, most of which was spent with Sara hiding her sexuality from the world and especially her parents. So, there I was keeping secrets in another part of my life.

When Sara took a job in another city, we stayed together, but it became a long-distance relationship. Our relationship shifted to mostly talking on the phone and I began to see our incompatibilities. I discovered it was easier to keep her secret when she wasn't around. In the meantime, I reconnected with a classmate from college and her girlfriend. A classmate who had been a dear friend early in our college days, and then she participated in outing me. I'm not sure I ever truly forgave her but when we reconnected and she was out and with a partner, I tried to let bygones be bygones and forgive.

It didn't take long before we were doing things together and hanging out. After all, we had horses in common. As far as they knew, I was single. What a great job I was doing of keeping Sara's secret. My classmate's girlfriend started calling me more frequently to check in and chat. We would talk and laugh on the phone. I resonated with her at every level, and looked forward to her calls. I would feel giddy inside every time we talked. When the three of us were together, I noticed I was getting more attention from Shelly than my former classmate, Shelly's partner. There was a definite attraction, but neither of us crossed the physical boundary. At the time, I thought I was being good, but if I'm being honest, we were having an emotional affair. I wasn't keeping my girlfriend's secret; I was keeping *her* a secret.

One spring day, I got a call from my former classmate that Shelly's mare had given birth and the foal died. She then said that her girlfriend, Shelly, needed me. I realized as I arrived and Shelly ran to my arms to be held, the truth of us, and clearly, so had my former classmate. Shelly ran into my arms crying and melted into my embrace burying her face in the side of my neck. It was an intimate moment meant for partners. I knew my classmate's and Shelly's relationship was over and felt a small glimmer of heat and hope. It was the first time I acknowledged my feelings for her to myself and in that moment I held her tightly in my arms with a deep love and caring in my heart.

I told Shelly about Sara, but she didn't care. Our affair was filled with laughter and joy. I felt a total freedom with her and looked for every second we could spend together. Sara thought I had developed a strong, new friendship, and she was right. I thought we were having a good time and didn't fully consider the future or how this might end. Shelly and I had so many things in common, especially the horses, and I just wanted to feel good with someone. We shared a lot of our time together. I juggled both relationships, thinking I was getting my cake and eating it too, but really, I was setting us all up for heartbreak and devastation. Consequences come eventually no matter what.

One year into my affair I began to feel guilty, especially after realizing how my feelings had deepened for Shelly. I really wanted to stop the deceit and focus on growing a future with Shelly, if possible. I wanted the guilt to end, along with the juggling, so I decided to fess up to Sara, who was currently visiting at my apartment. Crying, I told her everything, all the while hoping Sara would end our relationship. Instead, she forgave me and said that we would work it out. I caved in and thanked her for her forgiveness. It wasn't what I wanted, but I didn't have the maturity to end it myself. I had weaponized her heart.

I felt guilty and relieved after telling her but heartbroken about Shelly and the future I had been dreaming of with her. Shelly and I attempted to remain friends, but our hearts and bodies longed for one another. It was as if we were magnetized to each other physically, and our attraction, though well-hidden, never went away. I was heartbroken and resented Sara for forgiving me. Sara and I never truly recovered from my deceit.

While my personal life was a mess, I was thriving with the horses. My business was going gangbusters, and my reputation as a sought-after trainer was spreading. People would describe me as a horse whisperer, but that is not true. My secret weapon was that I was, am, a phenomenal horse *listener*. As a sex abuse survivor and thriver, I developed a heightened sensitivity to the energy in other beings and the ability to pick up on the subtlest shifts in behavior, intent, and emotion. I'd been honing those skills since that first experience at six years old. That encounter began a process of heightened awareness around others. Each trauma encounter thereafter refined my sensitivity and I turned that survival skill into a tool that served me in other aspects of my life including professionally.

My survival program evolved and developed with each predator encounter. I took that sensitivity and passion for horses and turned it into a skill set. As awful as those sexual assaults were to my body and psyche, they were also a gift as a trainer, instructor, and eventually a facilitator because I chose to turn lemons into lemonade. I utilized my enhanced sensitivities to help others instead of handicapping myself, and it is still an ongoing process and choice.

This skill allowed me to respond at a softer volume and either reward or redirect each horse I was working with. The like-language and trust I built with a horse would often create a super-soft and highly responsive mount—great for skilled riders but challenging for beginners. While I loved that my Tate horse would shift to a haunches-in with no more than a thought and a slight shift in weight, not all my clients desired that level of sensitivity. It took time and years of practice to train horses for clients who were not into such sensitivity. And still, I often failed at it. I guess it's like a singer with perfect pitch trying to sing off key; it's not really possible.

Eventually, I only took on horses in training for certain-caliber riders to do justice to both the horse and their partner. However, as an instructor specializing in partnership development, my ability to support and enhance riders developing their own horse exploded.

Tate proved a boon for my business in his own way. That horse and I could dance and flow. Unfortunately, the few times I let others ride him, both he and the rider would become frustrated, resulting in an unsatisfying experience for everyone involved. So, I stopped letting others ride him. But on the ground, he was as gentle as they came and became a master teaching horse from the ground and eventually as a co-facilitator.

Several years into my business I noticed an interesting pattern when people approached me to start their young horses. Whenever a woman would call, the conversation would inevitably end with them wanting to send the horse to some "cowboy" for the first thirty to sixty days because they didn't want me to get hurt, as if I were a fragile and breakable woman. Men, however, had no seeming problem sending horses to be started by me. This would have been a perfectly fine scenario and business model if it weren't for the fact that over 70 percent of horse owners are women. Eventually I began to resent this pattern and the women who were calling. I just could not understand why you would go to all that trouble and expense to get a bad start on your young horse, to then send the colt to me to spend even more money to fix all the problems and restart your horse.

Somehow, I related to male clients differently. It seemed easier to build a like-language with them. At the time I thought it was interesting, but from my decades-older perspective, I came to realize that likely two things were occurring: My sexual trauma had taught me a way to engage with males that didn't threaten them and created a sense of safety for both of us. Second, I believe I was so adept at recognizing predatory energy that I was subliminally only taking male clients who felt safe.

Sadly, I did not have the same programming in place with women. They could fool me. One such female client taught me one of my most valuable life lessons. I reached a point in my career where I had a solid reputation as a trainer. I had developed a rule early on that for any horse I had in training, the rider would be required to schedule a minimum of two lessons with me and their horse per thirty days of training. It was of the utmost importance for the rider to learn how I trained their horse and how to successfully communicate with said horse. At one point,

I was getting close to burnout but still taking whatever client came my way out of fear, buying into the idea that the business was feast or famine. The idea of my clients drying up and me going broke terrified me. After all, I had mouths to feed.

One day, a new prospective client approached me about starting a horse for her, and my internal alarm went off. She told me stories of how she had grown up riding and training, one story included solving a horse's behavior by using a two-by-four between their ears repeatedly. She was emphatic that she wanted to do things differently, and I gave in to my fear and took her on as a client. I had known her young horse as a foal and wanted to do right by her as well.

Back then and still today, if I take a horse for training, we go on each individual horse's timetable for development. Physical, mental, and emotional maturity must be taken into account when training a horse. I had that horse for ninety days, yet her canter just had not developed in a fully balanced way. She was big and gangly and an immature warmblood who, in my opinion, just was not ready for much canter work with a rider. She needed to build strength and confidence in her abilities and learn to balance better with a rider at lower gaits. The client took her home after ninety days of training, stating that she was happy with the outcome. Not long after, I learned that there had been no change in that owner's approach. Whenever things got a little challenging with the horse, out came the old ways of dominance and violence.

I felt so guilty that I had shown that horse a gentler, more patient, and partnership-focused approach, only to later let her go home with that abusive owner, that it changed me as a trainer. I was devastated that she was being abused and heartbroken. I felt as though I had failed her horse in every way possible. I wondered if I should show up at the client's home and reeducate her. I wondered if there was anything I could do to protect the horse. I realized there was truly nothing because I did not own her. I became so depressed and angry and frustrated that I hated humans and wanted nothing to do with any clients. After a few days I regained some perspective and new I couldn't leave all the horses in my care and in training hanging. I then made a life and career changing decision that scared the pants off of me.

I swore I would never take another client that my intuition said no to, whether I could afford to only eat ramen noodles or not. I just would not do it. That decision terrified me, but I knew I had to live by my shifted values. Lo and behold, that internal shift opened an energetic door, and clients who better aligned with my evolved values began to appear. It was one of the best lessons I've experienced, as well as one of the hardest. I'm grateful to that owner and horse to this day, though still a little sad and angry with myself that I failed the horse due to fear-driven choices.

One of my long-term clients told me one day that she had to retire her horse due to injury and was looking for a new riding horse. It was time for me to let go of Scarlet, begrudgingly, for financial reasons. I had several significant offers on the table but wanted the right of first refusal if her new owner decided at any point to sell her. Only one person was willing to honor my request. She was already a client, and I was familiar with her, so I chose to sell her Scarlet.

Scarlet was an amazing teacher for my client and friend. That horse taught her how to ride with confidence and to have a soft hand and subtle approach. My friend honored our agreement, and when the time came, Scarlet came back to me, and we remained together for the rest of her life. Tate, I never sold, and he remained with me to his dying day.

BUBBA

IN THE EARLY YEARS of my business, I developed a close friendship with a farrier and bull rider named Dennis, a wild, crazy guy and a good horseman. We ended up working young and problem horses together for a client. The two of us eventually became neighbors as he shared the house on a property attached to mine via a breezeway. We would party together, raise a little hell at night, and work horses during the day. The hardest part of my day was getting Dennis up in the morning to ride colts after he'd been out drinking—oh, and kick all those random women out of his bed to speed up the process.

We were like siblings, and that included our discourse. I loved Dennis. He was a good guy trying to heal a broken heart by partying and sleeping with lots of women. I resonated with his heartbreak and need to raise some hell to heal. We proved to be a good team and for several years leaned on one another through heartbreak and celebrations of success.

Before I moved in next to Dennis, I lived with my then-girlfriend, Anna, whom I had met while she was still in college. I was head over heels for her, but we were definitely at different places in our lives. Anna was younger than me by several years, but I fell for her hard and made the first move, asking her out. She agreed after several requests, and I fell in love. We were from very different worlds, but we clicked. She wasn't an animal person but supported me. She was very driven like me. I related to her drive and that's why I fell so hard for her. A college athlete, she played softball, volleyball, and basketball at the highest level in college. I've never met anyone who worked as hard as Anna.

We lived together for several years, but our differences in maturity and life experiences tore us apart. It was my turn karmically to experience being cheated on and Anna was the one to gift me that lesson. I thought we could work through anything and believed in a lifetime together with her. So when my gut kept telling me there was something hinky going on with her coworker, I simply asked her. She denied it, but continued spending more and more time with the woman.

Finally, one night at dinner—she always chose mealtimes for big conversations—Anna told me the truth. I was devastated, furious she had lied to me, and incensed that I had gone against my gut, all at the same time. My stomach turned upside down and I just didn't know what to say, so I cried and moved out. I knew she had so many lessons to learn and experiences to have that I had already gone through, and when we came apart, I moved in next door to Dennis.

I was heartbroken, my personal life a mess yet again, but business was thriving. One of my clients, who was married to a man, began hanging out more and more with me. She said she wanted to make sure I was okay and be there for me through my heartbreak. I thought nothing of it and was appreciative; after all, she was married. She would stay after her lessons and just talk with me.

Soon she started making me meals as she loved to cook. I thought it was a beautiful gesture from a friend who simply cared. I just never considered an ulterior motive on her part. I invited her to a gay bar with me and some friends to go dancing. She had mentioned wanting to go to the clubs with us and dance, so I innocently invited her. I'll never forget what she was wearing that night when I picked her up. I knew she had modeled but I remember thinking, Oh damn. Too bad she's married.

That night on the dance floor, at nearly closing time, I discovered that she was interested in more than friendship. We danced and flirted. I thought we were just having fun, and then she kissed me. It was not a peck on the cheek, she stopped in the middle of the floor, took my face into her hands and kissed me deeply and passionately. I was floored but sparks flew. I felt things for her in that moment that made me want her. We made out in the middle of the dance floor for a few minutes and when we got back to the table, my friends were sitting there with mouths agape. No one expected the evening to go that way.

I stopped things from going any further. I had recently experienced being cheated on by Anna—the straw that broke the camel's back for us and sealed our ending. I had also cheated and had an affair with a previous girlfriend and wasn't interested in creating that kind of heartbreak for someone else.

So, I resisted and told her we could only be friends. After a few months, Caroline decided to leave her husband and moved into her own place. I was truly smitten, and it wasn't long before we started dating and eventually moved in together. I believed it would be different this time. Looking back, I see the pattern: Many of my relationships occurred because the individual had pursued me. I was always caught off-guard by their pursuit. I found it flattering, and the attention fed things deep inside that I lacked, including self-love and worthiness. In my brain, the sexual trauma programming set me up to believe that pursuit meant love in some twisted fucking way. It doesn't make logical sense to me, but that is what happened.

My relationship with Caroline grew volatile at times. It was a relationship with an addict, which I didn't know she was dealing with, early on. She had shifted her addictive behavior to horses and riding instead of drugs, and I had not been in a relationship or around addicts prior to her. Things could go from good to horrible in a snap, and these snaps usually involved a night out with alcohol. One example occurred a few years into our relationship. We had gone to the club dancing, had a few drinks, and she had secretly done a few bumps of cocaine in the bathroom.

When we left, I asked if I needed to drive. She said no but seemed a bit agitated. I was uncomfortable letting her drive, but had discovered over the years that sometimes it was safer emotionally to give in. As we were nearing the end of our fifteen-minute commute home, she started yelling at me out of the blue for questioning her ability to drive. Screaming at the top of her lungs, she slammed on the brakes and then slapped the side of my face as hard as she could. I was stunned; my face stung like wind burn at its worst. My jaw hurt, and my left ear began to ring. Her slap made me bite my cheek and I felt the sting of the bite and blood filling my mouth. I didn't say a word the first time she slapped me; I was just too stunned.

Caroline would then hit the gas and take off, only to repeat the process within seconds. This experience happened between ten to twelve times in all that night. At first, I was too shocked to say anything and afraid my words might escalate her behavior. What if she decided to intentionally drive her car into a guard rail? After five or six times, I finally found my voice, but all I could do in the moment was say, "Please stop," and "Let's just get home safely."

Her actions repeated until we arrived at our front door. I was shaking with fear and shock, all I wanted to do was get out of that car safely and into the house. The last time she slapped me was beside the front door as I was putting the key in the lock to open the door to our house. I just couldn't take being hit one more time. My head and jaw were throbbing, tears were running down my cheeks, my fists were balled, and I was terrified if I responded in any way I might hurt her. That last slap was my final straw internally and somewhere deep inside I chose to act. I put my hand on her throat and pushed her against the wall. Her feet lifted off the ground. I just wanted her to stop hitting me.

Her eyes became huge and she started to cry. She told me how scared she was that I would hurt her, as if all the times she'd slapped me and nearly wrecked the car had not happened. I was gutted by my violence. I let go and dropped to my knees, I apologized over and over and felt so guilty. Guilty for protecting myself. And shame for not controlling my actions or anger. I spent days, even weeks, trying to make it up to her. Flowers, apologies, taking her out to dinner, anything she wanted. My worst fear had come true and I had put my hands on another person. What a twisted experience and total mind fuck.

I don't think it's uncommon for a survivor of trauma to feel this way. Guilt or shame for protecting oneself from violence. It took everything in my power to take action, finally. But the mental game got me, and instead of walking away, I stayed. Suddenly I was made out to be the abuser, not the victim defending myself. She cunningly flipped the script and had me groveling to her for forgiveness. She never apologized for slapping me, or yelling at me, or nearly wrecking the car multiple times that night.

How could I love this person and stay with them? Someone who lashed out and caused harm with words and physical violence? Someone who had triggered me to act in ways I had never wanted to act? I kept looking for the good in her and justifying her behavior. *It's the drugs. She's not normally like this. I'm sure I caused the response. She doesn't know how to cope with her feelings.* I took responsibility for not only my actions but also hers. It's insidious how the beliefs and programming born from childhood trauma took hold in my mind. With each violation, my mind told me it was my fault, bolstered by all the justification my shadow side could muster.

During my time with Caroline, I was introduced to Dennis' grandfather, a horseman in Northeast Kansas. I was looking for a horse for a client, and he had a nice dun quarter horse gelding for sale, a perfect first horse. I took my client up to try the gelding, and that was the first time I met Bubba. He was a four-year-old black and white paint stallion, and after five minutes I knew he had to be mine. I was so drawn to him—I just wanted to hang out with him and go for a ride. Instantly I knew our hearts belonged together. He was a beautiful young horse with good conformation and breeding. I offered to buy him, cash in hand.

"Girls don't need no stallion! But if your other client is interested in purchasing ten broodmares, I'll let him go in a package deal," Dennis' granddad said.

I was dumbfounded. I was a professional trainer, successful, and standing there with cash in hand, yet he said no simply because I wasn't male. I tried several ways to talk him into my deal as my client didn't want broodmares at the time, but to no avail. I drove away that day knowing he was slowly reducing his herd, and I couldn't purchase my boy. I felt deflated and confused by his stance. I had never in my life witnessed a horse trader turn down cash in hand.

The old man stood by his mistaken convictions and outdated beliefs. Dennis tried on my behalf to talk him into the sale, but the old man stood his ground. I walked away but never let go of the idea of Bubba. I held him in my heart and still hoped to buy him one day. A year after that no he told me, the old man sold Bubba to a guy without much horse experience and no breeding experience on a payment plan. WTF!

In the meantime, I took over a new barn as manager. The owner had never had horses, and his original manager had talked his way into the deal of a lifetime: onsite housing, a salary, and free care for his seven personal horses. I came into the picture looking for a new home for my business. The facility I'd worked out of had sold three times while I was there. Each owner had good intentions but no idea how to run a boarding business or care for a facility. I was invited to stay on and continue my business each time, but the last buyer, well, she was something else.

Apparently, she wanted me out, but instead of simply asking me to move on, she started a campaign to ruin my reputation and get rid of me. It took a few months for me to figure out what was going on. A client finally told me the new owner was spreading rumors about me being gay and how dangerous that was to clients and their families. My sexual orientation was not news to anyone; all my clients knew. I was not in the closet. But who I was within a relationship had nothing to do with me as a trainer. The rumors became nastier, all of which involved lies about my character and professionalism.

I was suddenly dropped right back into my experience of being outed at college and attacked. I felt so angry that I wanted to lash out. How dare she pull this kind of immature and juvenile behavior. Why couldn't she have simply asked me to move on? I did not understand her behavior, especially her need to be sweet and supportive to my face while bad-mouthing me behind my back. It made no sense to me. I began looking for a place to go after utilizing an attorney to get her to back off when I found the new barn.

I met with the owner of the new barn and began taking clients by to see the facility. It wasn't long before the owner realized it would be better to have me as his manager after discussing typical industry protocol and terms. It didn't hurt that my client list filled two-thirds of the barn. So, Caroline and I moved into the main house there, and I got started. The first year was busy, and my relationship with Caroline was slowly ending.

By year two at the new barn, I had deepened my friendship with Tina, one of my clients. We had already done some couples' activities together. Tina had been with her partner, who owned a house with her, for several years. The four of us would double-date and go out together for dinner periodically. The gelding purchased from Dennis' granddad was for Tina. We had been friends for years and had a number of friends in common. She had always wanted a horse. So, when the time came for her to purchase one, she came to me.

About a year into my tenure at this facility, Tina began flirting and pursuing more than a friendship. We danced around our attraction for a short while, but our attraction won. Once again, I was caught off guard by her interest in me but was also flattered by her desire. Mix this in with my longing to end my abusive relationship with Caroline and my lack of maturity, and *bam*. An affair began. Again, I simply moved on to someone new to get rid of someone I no longer wanted to be with. We cheated on our partners for a few months, then ended our other relationships and moved in together. Broken hearts resulted all around. Tina wanted so desperately to live her perception of my life that she missed the reality. And I just loved that feeling of new attraction and beginning love.

Tina embraced my lifestyle and work as a trainer, so when Dennis called one day with an offer for me to buy Bubba, I knew I had her full support, even in coming up with the cash in an hour. Dennis had called me out of the blue to tell me he was on his way to pick up Bubba or get the money owed. The guy who'd bought him on the payment plan had Bubba for the past year. He stood Bubba to outside mares and made money off him but had only made two initial payments on his purchase price. The old man had sent Dennis to get his money or his horse. Dennis said he wanted to bring Bubba straight to me and that "the old man doesn't need to know, if you're interested."

Oh my God, Bubba was finally going to be mine! I was caught off guard when Dennis had called, but my wheels began to turn immediately on how to get the money. I'm not sure I've ever been so excited and grateful in my life. I looked up into the heavens and thanked every deity I could think of, including the horse ancestors. I said yes to Dennis and then went to Tina to help pull the cash together with Bubba already on his way to me.

It had been two years since I first tried to purchase him, but I'd thought about Bubba every day, hoping for him to one day be mine. I had nearly given up by the time Dennis called. The universe can sure surprise us sometimes. Tina provided the cash from her savings along with what I had saved up. I promised to pay her back and did, but for that generous gesture, I will forever be grateful. My heart nearly stopped when Dennis pulled in and dropped him off, papers in hand. He just said, "I know you'll do something with him and honor his potential." I put Bubba in a stall with tears of joy streaming down my face. A new chapter began.

I had ridden and trained stallions by this point—quite a few actually—and knew what to expect. Stallions have the highest level of sensitivity among horses, physically, emotionally, and environmentally. In their natural habitat in a herd or family group, they fulfill a variety of roles, raising the young, reproducing, keeping their family band together, and protecting the herd from outside threats, including other stallions who might want to steal their mares; so, heightened sensitivity is necessary.

Bubba picked up on everything in his environment while at the same time remaining grounded and steady. He had stepped off that trailer with me at the lead and it was almost as if he said to me, "About time, what took you so long to bring me home?" The immediate challenge with him was that he had been allowed to become horse-aggressive with geldings. A natural instinct to protect his herd from other males. He was never aggressive to horses while under saddle, only when loose or led past a gelding who would taunt him.

That first winter, one of my staff forgot to close all the stall doors before leading him down the aisle, and a gelding taunted Bubba over a stall guard. Bubba dragged my staff member over to that stall with his ears pinned and teeth slightly bared. He was not having that gelding's sass and he dragged my grown staff person like she was a paper doll. Thanks to the grace of God, some last-minute boundary-setting that involved waving a stock whip in front of him, and the fact that the smartass gelding moved to the back of his stall, the situation didn't escalate.

My staff member recounted the story in a sweat with big eyes and extensive animation. It was an experience I doubt she'll ever forget. It was a great reminder that horses gift us their cooperation and to never forget they are bigger and stronger, and we are the weaker species. No horse or human was harmed in the incident, and no one forgot protocol with Bubba ever again!

Bubba and I worked hard on manners appropriate to our environment and began building a partnership. The guy who attempted to purchase him prior to my acquisition used some sketchy and frankly abusive techniques to manage his behavior. One technique was spraying Bubba with a water hose whenever he would vocalize in his stall at a horse going by. Thus, I had to deal with the aftermath: a very sensitive and fearful horse when it came to water being sprayed.

Baths took a while to feel safe for him, as did his stall. Each time I tried to take him into the wash rack he would go in and then drag me right back out with him. I tried everything to gently get him in and build his confidence, even treats, but he was never food motivated and frankly way bigger and stronger than me. He would also notice horses coming down the aisle when in his stall, and as they walked by, he would just jump to the back of his stall, anticipating getting sprayed. I educated everyone on how to respect his space and set clear boundaries of engagement outside his stall. There was to be no stopping and peering at him, no stopping with a horse directly in front of his stall, and his water bucket was filled by hand for several months before we started using a hose. It took time to help him through this issue. I reminded everyone how he behaved inside the stall was his business. This approach worked. He eventually became quiet and secure in his stall, relaxed even.

The power of listening to the horse's behavior as feedback instead of labeling it as "bad" had a profound positive impact. When the weather warmed from spring to summer, I started teaching him how to be rinsed outside the barn with a long hose. I would gently spray a foot, he would move around evading, and I would keep spraying until he stopped and stood. At that point I would turn the water off. Once he settled, I would start again. His terror began to resolve and his flight instinct lessen as we built trust through this gentle and gradual approach. Eventually, he was fine with washracks and baths, and validation occurred for me around my gentle approach. Dominance had been preached and taught as the preferred and necessary way to handle a stallion. I was proving that theory wrong.

I was over the moon to finally have Bubba, and my heart was filled with love and joy from the first moment I took his lead rope in my hand. Dennis facilitated a heavenly gift by selling me that horse. I don't know whether he ever told the old man. Several years down the road, I had the opportunity to explain to Dennis what a life-changing and heart-fulfilling moment it was when he drove up my drive and dropped off my dream horse. He shared with me that he had followed our journey and was very proud of us both. He said that he made the right decision that day, and I agreed, wearing a Cheshire cat-sized grin on my face.

I made a few surprising discoveries when I first started riding Bubba. He was hard in the mouth and was ranch-trained, and whenever he got stressed, he would rear. Dennis had told me he caused the rearing by starting Bubba under saddle with too much pressure to advance him quickly. So, I went back to the beginning and did everything as if starting him from scratch. This gave me the opportunity to find any holes in his training and plug them.

It only took about three months before he was riding really well and soft in my hands. The one behavior that lingered his entire life was the rearing. But here's the deal: He would rear in slow motion. He'd shake his head slowly as a warning, then collect himself and lift his front end until he was at three-quarters his standing height. He would then hold himself there for several seconds and slowly paw the air; once the motion was complete, he would lower himself back to the ground slowly and fully in control. The strength it took him physically to lift and move his body this way is unbelievable.

My inner child secretly thought this was the greatest thing ever. Suddenly, I was back in Garden City watching the Royal Spanish Riding School trainers riding their stallions and demonstrating a move similar to Bubba's rear. Decades later my dreams came true; I had my very own spectacular stallion, he did at least one movement like a war horse. Those years riding Chief and handling his rearing had prepared me for Bubba decades later.

Owning, campaigning, and standing a stallion always made sense to me from a professional standpoint. Looking back, I can see the healing and reframing that occurred for me around male energy. As stereotypical as Bubba was as a stallion in his masculinity and machismo, he was also soft and gentle just like my dad.

My father was a hardworking man, intelligent, kind, and caring. Animals were drawn to him, and I think that says a lot about who he was. Dad wasn't all machismo or a manly man, just really balanced in his yin/yang energy, my model for safe, masculine energy. Males who were domineering or macho never felt safe to me. This was enhanced by my experiences of being victimized and sexually assaulted. I didn't expect some of the lessons I received from Bubba, a very machismo horse, to change my relationship with masculinity. But he did.

As the person who handled the breeding stallion, it was my responsibility to maintain the mare's safety along with that of the stallion. Often, in a traditional breeding environment, mares would wear breeding hobbles, a device that prevented the mare from kicking and harming the stallion during breeding and mounting. You know, protecting the money-maker on the stallion, as it were.

The thing is, people would often hurry the process, breeding mares before they were fully ready. My brain experienced this as rape. Now I'm not saying it is or judging anyone who utilizes breeding hobbles. I'm referring to my trauma-based perspective. So, I refused to run my breeding operation that way and would not use them. Because of this stance, I had to tease the mares until I was certain they were fully in heat and receptive to live cover by my stallion. In return, I had to ensure that Bubba had impeccable manners with the girls because he could get kicked and seriously injured. I have to say that it did not take much boundary-setting for him to elevate his behavior to worthy of breeding a mare.

I used Scarlet to train him, and he adored her. I really wanted a foal from the two of them but was determined to honor what she wanted as she had not really liked being a mom. So, I turned her loose in a small indoor arena and had Bubba on a long line. He started off very excited and was a bit pushy. She pinned her ears, kicked at him without contact as a warning, and then trotted off. This scenario happened twice. The third time, she kicked him in the side with a pretty good thwap and trotted off. I watched her intentionally set boundaries with him, escalating a bit more each time when he didn't honor her needs or respond quickly enough for her. I had him on a line the entire time and could manage his behavior, if need be, but really, I let Scarlet retrain him.

After the last kick, it seemed she'd hurt his feelings or pride. Either way, his next approach was as slow as possible and respectful. He lowered his head to the ground, would take a step or two toward her, and then nickered gently, repeating this process across the entire arena, until she allowed him to reach her. He then stood next to her, sniffing and nuzzling her starting at her neck and working his way back to her flank while honoring each tail swish or ear flick as a boundary. If she pinned an ear, he stopped. If she snaked her head, he stopped. If she swished her tail at him or cocked a hip, he stopped. He took his time and romanced her until she was ready. That final approach took thirty minutes.

Finally, she allowed him to mount and breed her. She didn't take and never showed interest in being bred again by him. I was fine with that outcome. More importantly, what she did provide was a life lesson for him as a breeding stallion that changed his behavior. She also taught me what it looked like to set boundaries in an intimate or sexual setting. I had no idea what it felt like to have "No" honored by a male in a sexual sense. Or what it looked or felt like to be female and in control of a sexual experience with a male in such a natural, self-care focused way. The entire time I owned Bubba, I only bred mares when they were ready by choice.

Bubba and I were together for eighteen years, and he saw me through several relationships. Tina and I weren't a great fit. Looking back, I can see the pattern. When someone pursued me with an intense focus, quite dysfunctional, I thought it was love and would go along with it. Now to be fair, I was attracted to them in return. Tina and I wanted a similar lifestyle, which wrapped around horses and living on a horse property. Eventually, we purchased a farm with a friend of hers named Amanda who would periodically come and stay with us. Interestingly, Tina and I both had a history of cheating on our partners, and I guess it was her turn to experience the other side.

After the three of us moved to the farm, Amanda and I started spending more time together. There had been an attraction prior, but nothing had occurred between us. One weekend, Amanda and I were alone at the farm; we started the weekend with coffee on the deck and light flirty conversation. I felt drawn to her, wanting to sit as close as possible. I laughed a little too loud at her stories and focused on catching her eyes in mine, only to stare deeply into them before she looked away.

I had lessons to teach that morning, and when I stood

to get ready, I offered to take her dishes. When I reached for her coffee cup our hands glanced. I froze for an instant feeling the vibration of physical attraction and desire course through my body. When I began to move my hand away, she quietly reached out to my arm and suggested we have drinks later and talk, as her hand caressed my arm. I spent the rest of the day unfocused and thinking about her touch. After drinks that night we found our way into one another's arms and then her bedroom.

We spent the weekend in bed around chores and talked nonstop when we weren't otherwise engaged. I hadn't talked to a romantic partner like this since my first serious girlfriend. I felt a bit guilty, but really, I had moved forward with the farm and Tina only because that was what I wanted and the wheels were in motion, not because I wanted to stay in that relationship.

Honestly, I kind of thought relationships were supposed to become crappy at some point, that it was the norm. I made some immature decisions that impacted several people's lives in a really shitty way, and for the pain I caused, I'm truly sorry. But at the time, I thought I was choosing love and forever with Amanda. Eventually, I broke up with Tina, and we all decided to move forward with the partnership on the property. I can only speak to how that felt for me, and it was uncomfortable as hell, but I had the farm and plenty to do. I was just busy doing my horse thing and being in love with no regard to how it affected anyone around me.

Amanda and I talked about marriage and having a family.

We proposed to one another the same night and went ring shopping that weekend. I was blissfully in love and excited for our future together.

Amanda was part Native American and we decided on a native-influenced commitment ceremony in Colorado in a friend's teepee with a dozen people in attendance. I invited my mom and two of my brothers and their spouses, along with two couples we'd befriended through the horses. Amanda's sister was invited and attended, but her parents refused to attend. Amanda wasn't fully out of the closet until that point, and when she told her mother and father, it did not go well initially. She was heartbroken but refused to let narrow-minded beliefs get in the way of her forever. I was really proud of her for moving our wedding forward in spite of her disappointment.

Our wedding was like a dream come to life. The hand-made traditional teepee of deer skins rested on top of the Colorado Divide. A fire was kept burning in the center providing warmth and a distinct smokey pine scent wafting upward and out the vented top. On the way from our B&B to the ceremony, we stopped to watch the largest herd of elk I had ever seen cross the road. The size and power of the herd was awe-inspiring. Snow crunched under their feet as they walked along the side of the road, steam pluming from their nostrils. We felt as though the elk were a good omen.

The snow shone on the mountain peaks and all along the skyline. Our officiant guided us through a tobacco ceremony blessing our guests. I felt so connected with Amanda that day that I couldn't imagine a life without her. We wore wool sweaters for the ceremony and for months after our wedding, every time I opened the closet where they were stored, I could smell a hint of smoke from our teepee ceremony, warming my heart and making me smile. We were in love and living a fairy tale.

Professionally, I was thriving. A client gifted me *The Tao of Equus* by Linda Kohanov, insisting I read the book because the contents seemed so similar to my life—how I worked with clients and horses. After the first ten pages, I cried tears of resonance. I couldn't believe I wasn't the only person out there helping people through life and lessons with horses in this unique way.

My clients had been utilizing our partnership lessons, practiced with their horses, home to their human relationships. The correlation between building a like language with a horse and the spouse at home seemed a no-brainer to me, but clients were surprised at how effective and life-changing those lessons could be with humans. I saw clients save relationships and change family and work dynamics for the better through lessons learned with a horse. It was profound and empowering to be a small part of people's growth.

I was intrigued by the book and discovered the author and her business partner at the time, Kathleen Barry Ingram, were training people on how to do their version of such work. I signed up for their apprenticeship, which changed my path and life. The program lasted a year, with five separate weeks of onsite learning spent in Arizona.

I discovered many things that year through my training, such as shamanism, the importance of peer support, and how much I love working with people through that horse-as-teacher model. It had been some time since I had been immersed in new learning in this way. The distance learning was right up my alley, practicing new techniques with horses and clients, which really weren't far off from what I was already doing. The onsite portion, which was at Linda's ranch, was a total immersion in discomfort and vulnerability, partnered with personal growth and excitement.

My first time experiencing "the work" was with an appaloosa stallion Linda owned. He was white with spots all over his body and as gentle a horse as I have ever witnessed. He had been a breeding stallion on a large ranch that allowed their stallions to participate in a more natural herd environment. He had lived in bachelor bands and when his foals were weaned, they were moved to a pasture with him to help raise them and shape behavior. He was the most balanced stallion in his masculine and feminine energies. I was facilitated in a "Heart's Desire" experience where, after a guided meditation into self, and dialogue with my body and heart, I chose a heart's desire to experience with this horse—something that I could work towards experiencing together with him. What came to the surface for me was comfort, and I had no idea how that might look.

I entered a small round pen with the stallion loose; he watched me quietly as I entered. My inner dialogue was busy with thoughts of performance demands as I was a trainer—I did not know how to simply be in that pen without a performance goal. I was truly vulnerable as my peers watched and held loving space for my highest good. When I acknowledged to myself finally how conflicted and out of my comfort zone I felt, a quiet sigh of release came forth. At the same time the stallion began to yawn, lick and chew, and then gently walked toward me. All thoughts were gone from my mind as his nose nudged my arm. I placed my hand upon his neck and lightly began to stroke him. In that moment I felt utter peace as tears rose up from the deepest corners of my soul and fell from my eyes.

After a few minutes, he gently wrapped his head and neck around me and I leaned into his shoulder feeling comforted and safe in every cell of my body. When I got out of my head, and my own way, I experienced my heart's desire gifted to me from a profound and gentle stallion. This was a new lesson in gentle compassion and support provided by a male. He modeled kindness in a way that had only been shown to me by my father on the human side, a stark contrast from the males who had dominated and victimized me.

I also made lifelong friends from around the globe at that ranch in Arizona; there, I thrived. Upon graduation, I was invited to be a peer facilitator for the following year's class. Throughout that next year, I ran my business in Missouri while simultaneously working with apprentices, travelling to Arizona for another five weeks for classes. I was thriving and working my ass off. I could not have done any of it without the loving support of my wife, Mom, and my best friend Sue who managed and ran the farm while I traveled back and forth for two years.

By the end of the second apprenticeship, though, Amanda was unhappy in our farm arrangement. I allowed her displeasure and pressure to get to me, eventually reaching out to Linda. She had offered me a position when she purchased her new facility, but I was committed to our farm arrangement and making it a go at the time. Now, I was ready to make some changes, especially if it eased some conflict in the house and my discomfort.

Looking back, I realize I was being what Bubba had modeled in some ways when he received his lesson from Scarlet. I was tiptoeing and responding to every little thing as a boundary and just trying to keep the peace. Utilizing a warped and child-like perspective, I decided that the best choice was to get out of the business partnership and move on instead of standing and fighting for what I wanted. I could have taken those lumps and fought to buy Caroline out, but instead, I fled to where the grass seemed greener—well, it was the desert, but the cliché still stands.

I don't want to blame trauma here, but the truth is, I hadn't healed emotionally and was still stuck in those same immature patterns and belief systems. I can only see that now, looking back. At the time, however, I was doing the best I could. Therapy isn't instantaneous when healing. It takes time—apparently, in my case, lots of time—to develop emotional maturity and to change those deeply held patterns.

Linda hired me as the assistant farm manager, and Amanda and I headed to Arizona with my mom in tow. It was a decision we made as a family. Mom had been diagnosed with breast cancer and had a mastectomy in Kansas City right before we moved. We explored treatment options in Arizona and ultimately found a better chemotherapy protocol at University Medical Center in Tucson. So, with the decision made, and the appropriate people informed, we headed to Tucson with our horses in tow.

We found a place in Sierra Vista with five acres where we fenced two pastures, a larger one for the herd with Tate and Scarlet included, and a smaller one for Bubba. Because of Mom's chemotherapy schedule, which included twenty-two sessions, I worked a four-day schedule except during the facilitation of apprenticeship classes. At that point, I had a ninety-minute drive to and from work. While I thrived working with people, solving problems, and working horses on-site, my relationship with my own horses suffered. I just didn't have the time or energy for them at that point.

My herd didn't seem any worse for wear. They were curious about the border patrol flying low over the property hunting for people who'd crossed the border illegally, and the dogs were entertained by the people walking past all the time. All the animals were playful and relaxed in their environment. I was the one who suffered from a significant shortage of time with them. Maybe if we could have lived closer to my workplace, things would have been different.

Living without my horses, or more importantly, not having time to spend with them, impacted my heart and soul in a sad and dark way.

I met a woman, Andi, through the apprenticeship who asked if I would consult on a horse property in California. We thought it would be a nice, relaxing, long weekend for Amanda and me, so I agreed, and we headed for California. We stayed with Andi while there, and on Saturday, the three of us went to lunch after looking at a property. Amanda got up from the table, stating that she needed some air and didn't feel quite right.

I followed her out of concern, and as we reached the entrance, she collapsed on the floor and had a grand mal seizure in the middle of the lobby. It was the first time I remember as an adult being stunned and frozen, incapable of taking action. I just didn't know what was happening to my wife or what to do. My thoughts raced in circles with dark thoughts driven by fear and death. Andi stepped in and told someone to call an ambulance and to roll her onto her side. The ambulance arrived, which Andi and I followed to the hospital.

Amanda was admitted after a few hours in the ER. I was stunned. Our life had just changed in ways I couldn't imagine. More importantly we eventually learned there were treatment options, and that Amanda would be okay. By the time we left California several days later, we already had some answers and a game plan but were both shocked and terrified by what our future might hold.

Amanda was diagnosed with epilepsy and started on meds that made her sleep hours upon hours a day as she adjusted. The consequences of her seizure meant she couldn't legally drive for a designated number of months. I added "chauffeur" to my credentials and a slew of doctor's appointments for her to my already very packed schedule. My mom was doing great and feeling really well at this point, but Amanda wouldn't allow anyone to drive her but me. I pulled myself together and got to work balancing all my responsibilities and demands, but in truth I was avoiding conflict and out of fear, I was doing whatever she asked. At some point resentment began creeping in through cracks in my armor. By the end of our one year in Arizona and all the stress, we had decided to go back to the farm in Missouri as it hadn't sold and she had family closer to us.

Our relationship felt a bit one-sided to me. That might seem selfish, but it was the truth, and not the first challenge we'd faced around her health. On top of all our challenges she was determined to have children biologically. She did not want to adopt. I tried to get on board, but the level of risk for her pregnancy was very real, and I was not interested in being a single parent. She had also started chiropractic school, so our life was filled with things other than us. I was attempting to rebuild my business at the time as well. It was challenging, to say the least, as the housing bubble had burst and people weren't spending much money on horses. The one really good thing was how happy my herd was back on grass and how content I was to have ample time for them.

No matter what was going on, I could go to my horses for healing and peace. Bubba became my respite from everything. He was my saving grace, my angel. I would just go out, saddle him, and off we'd go. My time in the saddle with him was when I felt complete in my heart and soul. He would walk, and I would just breathe into my body and be present and content. I would tell him how much I missed working with people at the ranch in Arizona and socializing with my friends there. I told him how frustrated I was in my relationship and how unheard I felt. I told him my dreams for my business and life. I spoke of everything through tears and laughter, and he listened without judgment or advice. He was just there, my rock, my partner. I felt safe with him in body, mind, and soul.

The thing is, I should have been telling all these things to my wife. I couldn't somehow, and when I tried, I felt as though she never heard me. Nothing felt about me or us, and I didn't or couldn't successfully communicate what I was feeling. All that therapy and healing work over the years, and I couldn't find my voice in my marriage. So, when Andi called from California, telling me she'd purchased a property and asking whether I'd be interested in coming on board, I said I'd have to talk to my wife about it. I wasn't sure about moving again, but Amanda was all for it, and so the planning began.

TATE, SCARLET, AND DUNCAN

TATE WAS MY FUNNY, athletic boy from day one. I started him as a two-year-old, and he was so easy to train. He rode just like all those babies I rode down in Texas for Jack. He was also quite sensitive under saddle, which I loved. That made him a challenge for the few others privileged to have sat on his back. I not so secretly loved that about him and would use that to justify not sharing him. The first decade we were together, I felt I needed an excuse to keep him to myself. After that, I stopped caring—he was mine to ride, and mine alone.

I dreamed of Tate being a top reining horse and breeding stallion, though neither was his destiny. Gelding him was the right decision, yet I still hoped he'd become a reiner. He had it all: athleticism, looks, flash, and smarts, and much to my avail, he loved to jump. Jumping was his dream but not his future. That not-so-minor injury to his tendons and fetlock at two weeks old meant no jumping as a career. It was the first time I couldn't let a horse choose their path. To provide longevity and a pain-free life, I had to say no. When he was four and mostly finished growing, I would ride him English one day a week. We would do trot poles and low cross poles to build strength, which he loved. It broke my heart to stop him from jumping. He just always had that extra little spark when we'd soar over fences of any height.

He did not want to be a reining or even a show horse. He hated trail riding but would go out periodically. He was super-sensitive and hypervigilant, so trails were over-stimulating for him. He noticed anything and everything everywhere. On the trail, if a blade of grass moved in the wind, he noticed with a sudden stop and a snort. Nothing I did seemed to help. He really seemed happiest when it was just him and me, playing together in an arena, although he did like chasing after cows.

Tate was the most athletic and talented horse I never showed. His sensitivity and our like language from his birth meant we became like one when I rode him. I could tilt my hip, and he would go haunches-in with the subtlest of cues. It was truly as if we had a telepathic connection. We danced together. So many breathtaking rides with him exist in my memories that no one else saw, and what beautifully breathtaking memories they are. Moments and feelings of pure connection through body and mind, horse and rider gliding and dancing through gaits and dressage movements to the music in my head. Such profound joy I found in our partnership of hearts. He was so playful and powerful, it felt as though I was riding an almost always contained but overfilled helium balloon. But Tate's truest calling was as a facilitation horse.

When I took the job with Andi in California, I brought my herd with me—a partial win for both Andi and me since my herd was experienced and trained as facilitation horses.

Amanda decided to stay in Missouri for the summer and take classes before transferring to a program in California. I looked for a place for us to live while I resided on Andi's ranch property. I thought being apart from Amanda would be hard, but I discovered during my first few weeks in California that I felt as though I could breathe again. My thought at the time was that I just needed a little space.

Throughout our first client programs with the horses in California, Tate was a superstar—steady, safe, curious, engaged, and connected with every client he worked with. He was Mr. Go-To whenever we needed and was at the gate for every program. He *loved* people and engaging with them. He provided so many profound lessons for our clients. I'm sure, even today, photos of him stand on many desks as a touchstone to life-changing moments in the round pen. Moments that were like my first experience with that spotted stallion in the desert of Arizona, a profound and unexpected life-altering moment with a horse.

Scarlet went to California too, but her eyesight had begun to degenerate. She could still see pretty well when we arrived but preferred having company and seemed settled in her surroundings when she was with Duncan, an amazing buckskin gelding I had agreed to take years earlier at a clinic in North Carolina. He'd been purchased by a repeat clinic client who loved buckskins, but Duncan had proved a poor fit for her since he hadn't been started properly or well.

The story I heard from my client was that the folks up on the mountain had decided to start him themselves after watching some how-to videos. My client spent a lot of money on training for Duncan after bringing him home and discovering that he always bucked at a canter. Her trainer couldn't get him worked through it. So, she'd ultimately offered him to me. I agreed to buy him and turn him into a facilitation horse. He didn't have to be a riding horse if it wasn't for him, but I told her I would figure that out. I took him back to Missouri and turned him out for a few months with my herd.

After I brought Duncan back up, I explored his riding needs and started over from scratch like I would any problem horse. He had a few holes in his training, which I resolved. The big thing was that if he thought you were going to canter, he would get so tense and wound up that bucking seemed imminent. I figured he had experienced so much pain and trauma around the canter that I almost didn't care if he ever cantered again under saddle. I would let him choose to canter when he was ready, and after about nine months of riding, he did just that. After several strides into that first canter, it was like he realized what he'd done and immediately tensed up, sped up to a gallop, and then after a thundering lap, stopped. I just sat there and let him settle until he was ready to quietly walk off after decompressing.

He began cantering more frequently and would always respond in the same way. I never corrected or scolded him, I just allowed his process. It took months before I would ask him to canter, and he never became completely relaxed while doing so, but he did grow more comfortable with it and would gently lope most of the time. I was asked by a number of clients why I bothered even working on cantering under saddle since he was so problematic during the process. I told them that it was all about safety in the beginning. I needed him to respond to the rider without panicking and running off, thus getting himself or a rider hurt. I needed him to be able to resist tipping into panic flight as he truly enjoyed riding, and especially on the trails.

Duncan was Mr. Trail Horse. He loved riding out anywhere and was safe for anyone to ride on the trails. Because we'd done canter work, I wasn't worried he'd buck and it wasn't a gait he would choose on the trail, so I could let others ride him. He was a great teacher and confidence-builder on the trail. When we got to California, Andi, who hadn't ridden regularly in more than a decade, wanted to improve her riding skills. The few horses she'd personally bought were great at facilitation but not ideal riding horses for her. Duncan became that horse. Andi would ride him while I would ride Bubba out on the trails and around the ranch property. Her biggest complaint about Duncan was that he would go anywhere, even if there wasn't a trail. You could always see it in his body language when he was about to go off-trail adventuring. He would get a little bounce in his step and his ears would perk up, like a kid embarking on a great adventure.

Andi and I hit it off from the beginning. As different as we were, and despite our disparate backgrounds, we were sympatico when developing and facilitating programs together. She had started life in Philadelphia in a Jewish community before relocating to Scottsdale, Arizona as a teen, where her dad got her a job at a prominent Arabian horse farm to make amends to his daughter for selling her horse and moving. She had been in Southern California running her team and leadership company and raising two sons for two decades when we met. Our worlds collided in a beautiful way.

That summer without Amanda, I questioned everything about our relationship. Andi was there as a friend and sounding board and seemed truly concerned. Our friendship deepened, and she suggested that I consider whether I wanted to remain in that relationship. She facilitated me with horse sessions, and I did the same for her on a regular basis. We built trust in one another as co-facilitators and, if I'm being honest, it felt like more. She had only been intimate with men and would tell me she was straight while at the same time flirting with me. She kissed me one morning while we were joking around in the barn doing morning chores—I was still married to Amanda. She confused and surprised me, but deep down I desired the life I was sharing with Andi. It came with a feeling of freedom, mutually supportive, and partnership. She said she was experimenting after that kiss, but the *what-if* lingered for me.

At summer's end, I flew back to Missouri to drive Amanda and the rest of our stuff out to California. I didn't talk to her about my desire to end things until I got there. It just seemed like she never had time when we talked long-distance, and I didn't push it wanting to avoid conflict and heartbreak. Looking back, I see the pattern and the link to my trauma response, though I was blind to it at the time. The other side of that coin was Andi encouraging me to choose a life of freedom.

I finally told Amanda I wanted to end things after I arrived in Missouri. She decided to move to California anyway, so I drove us out to the apartment I'd set up but never lived in. I broke her heart because I wasn't mature enough emotionally to be in that relationship. I hadn't truly found my voice with Amanda and was making choices to keep the peace and make her happy until I couldn't. What I didn't understand at the time was that my skull fracture wasn't the true culprit in stealing my voice; when it came to relationships, that culprit was my trauma.

It didn't take long for things to evolve intimately with Andi. After I returned home, she shared her joy over my choice to end my relationship with Amanda and made it clear that she wanted to explore a same-sex relationship with me.

After our first intimate encounter, she told me it was the first time in her life she had felt safe in a sexual encounter and could be herself. In the beginning she was in the closet to everyone including her adult children. It was uncomfortable for me, but I was trying to honor her personal needs and the journey of discovering her sexuality. After all, I had been outed and the pain and loss that came with that experience was real. I did not wish that on anyone. I was willing to see where things went but said she would have to tell her boys if things continued to evolve. I was willing to be private but not in the closet indefinitely. Within my first year living in California, she told her boys, and at the time I thought that would be enough.

On the business side, we were thriving. Our ability to co-facilitate proved life-changing. We shared a passion for helping people and horses, lived on the property together, had deep and powerful conversations, and shared a bed and daily life. It felt really good that first year. When no one was around it felt like a true partnership in a loving happy relationship. Just us in our happy little bubble of life on the ranch. Morning coffee on the porch overlooking the property, shared mealtimes, laughter, shared chores, great discussions, and so much more.

We talked about adding to the herd. After all, we only had one mare onsite: Scarlet. We both felt we needed more feminine energy to balance out the herd dynamics. Andi had spent several formative years working with Arabian horses, and that included some of the top Arabian stallions in the world, one of whom was Bask, the famous bay stallion. I was very interested in crossing Bubba with a Russian- or Polish-bred Arabian to see what that combination would create. So, we began scouring the West Coast for the right fit.

THE GIRLS

WE CAME ACROSS AN AD for a herd liquidation of Arabian horses in Northern California. We reached out and discovered that many of the horses were of Crabbet and Bask descent, two highly regarded and sought-after bloodlines. There were a dozen mares we wanted to evaluate. Plans were made to go North with my horse trailer and come home full. The couple who owned the herd of forty-plus horses researched our business and agreed to hold the mares we were interested in until our arrival a month later after the rainy season.

When we got there, we met an older couple who'd spent their lifetime breeding, raising, showing, and loving this line of horses. The female owner had been diagnosed with an aggressive form of Parkinson's disease and was degenerating quickly, and her husband had had a double lung transplant a few years prior. They were spending all their retirement income on feeding and caring for their beloved herd. They shared with us that the ad they'd run, which included the phrase "$500 and up for pricing," had brought all the killer buyers out. The husband had run aggressive parties off with a shotgun because they wanted to buy horses to ship for meat. They were doing their best to keep up with everything in a devastating scenario of the cruelty of both of their medical conditions. I cannot imagine facing their outcomes and loss of their beloved herd with more grace and tenacity.

We stayed two full days in the rain and knee-deep mud, so much for the end of the rainy season, working with the mares we wanted to see. Some had been ridden, some shown with titles, some broodmares, some barely halter broke, and some never touched. They had a small round pen where I worked with each horse to test their ability to respond, connect, and become facilitation horses to work with clients.

The first I chose was a mare named Gypsy, very small in stature and seemingly a bit plain until she started to move; that's when she took our breath away with her awe-inspiring gaits and a deep connection to whoever worked with her. For me it was a no brainer to take her. Second was a three-year-old, breathtaking bay mare who was only halter broke. Third was the woman's favorite horse, which Andi fell in love with at first glance, named Mel. Mel had numerous titles and had produced winning offspring.

Last was a little mare they called a devil horse who looked almost exactly like the great Arabian stallion Bask. She seemed wild and very sensitive. She had lost her first foal and kept her second foal close by her side. They couldn't catch or touch her and were worried about me going in with her as they were sure she would attack me. They had hesitated even showing her to us because they were so convinced of her danger. They reiterated to us how likely it was I would get hurt if I went in with her and really thought we shouldn't bother. She was the one horse they considered selling to a killer buyer. She was six years old at that time.

I acknowledged their concern, ensuring them I was capable of maintaining my safety and would not hold them responsible if anything were to happen to me. I trusted in my skills and intuition. I walked into the paddock with her and the foal, an eight-month-old colt that they had tried to wean but gave up after he'd jumped the fence back in with her. The mud was above my calves, and I said a little prayer to the universe, placing trust in my experience.

It took me ninety minutes to reach her using a boundary technique where I stopped and consciously released energetic pressure every time I felt or even thought she was setting a boundary with me. It was a honed version of the technique Bubba had used years earlier with Scarlet, refined through a similar technique I learned at Epona with Linda. The technique worked because, ultimately, I was communicating in horse language through my gestures and breath, and she could understand me. I was able to reach and stand three feet off her left side near her head.

This was the moment of truth. I exhaled into the ground and looked away from her, showing absolute trust and vulnerability, just like I had seen horses do with one another numerous times. She reciprocated by reaching her nose over and smelling my neck and cheek, when I looked back at her she looked away from me bearing her neck in a sign of vulnerability and trust back. We successfully spoke horse to one another in that moment. We both exhaled and just stood there, both more relaxed, looking at each other. When I felt she was willing, I slowly and gently reached out and touched her neck with the back of my hand. She stood still, I exhaled and turned and walked away as she watched me go not moving an inch. I told Andi we couldn't leave without her; we held a positive and loving future for her when likely no one else did. And so, we had our four girls.

The next day, we loaded three mares with the agreement that I would come back for the devil mare. We got her in a stall and her colt in the stall next to hers. We wanted the separation and weaning restarted, and I felt I needed to come back for her so she could have the trailer to herself as she wasn't halter broke. So that's exactly what I did. I picked her up one week after we'd left the first time. I backed the trailer up to the barn and told her out loud we were going to her new safe home. I described our ranch to her and told her the other girls were waiting there already.

When I opened the stall door expecting a bit of a challenge and drama, she quietly looked around and walked out and onto the trailer. Everyone watching was dumbfounded. We called her Afire. I got her home and let her settle in. After a few days, I started building trust by just hanging out with her, approaching and then retreating, and eventually gently touching her body where she would allow. Two weeks after she came home, Andi gently slid a halter on her head, and she was leading in no time.

Those mares taught me some valuable lessons about resilience and second chances, none as much as Afire. She lived up to her label in Northern California because that was the only way they could see her. Because of that, any attempts to handle or manage her were done out of fear and quite aggressively. She'd been chased around relentlessly, scared into pens, had gates slammed on her, and been hit as a means to control—all done out of the fear of others to protect themselves from her. The only thing she could live up to was the label they had given her, a self-fulfilling prophecy of their making, not hers.

As a kid I had been labeled poor by some of my classmates, queer in college as if it were a bad thing, and too masculine as an adult female because I worked a physical job and was proud of my strength. All labels that were singular perceptions of a very complex being. Sometimes all it takes to lift the chains is someone willing to see us in all our diverse and glorious authenticity until we can do so for ourselves. In those moments of complex darkness, when I've been on my knees drowning in labels and self-doubt, a single, loving voice from the outside reminding me I'm worth fighting for has been the light I've needed to find myself again and rise. Each time breaking the chain of my own acceptance and self-doubt.

Afire became one of the most impactful facilitation horses in our herd, touching numerous lives in the gentlest of ways. I thought we were her gift and savior, but really, she was one of ours. After a while, Duncan grew tired of being Scarlet's companion and seeing-eye horse, and Afire chose to step into that role in his place. She would hang out with

Scarlet across the fence almost constantly, grooming one another and just hanging like besties.

The mares hadn't been on the best of feed before we acquired them and needed extra support nutritionally. Often poor nutrition and long-term stress does significant damage to the nervous system and digestive tract of a horse, which was the case with one of the mares we brought home. We lost her within two months to colic and a twisted intestine. The three remaining mares—Gypsy, Mel, and Afire—were thriving, and the following spring we bred them to Bubba fulfilling a mutual dream with Andi.

Eleven months later, out of our three solid-colored Arabian mares, we had three very flashy half-pinto Arabian fillies. Afire's baby was named Isis after the goddess, Mel's baby was named Athena after the goddess, and Gypsy's baby was named Cleopatra, or Cleo for short, after the strong Empress. Those babies brought a renewed energy to the property and to Andi's and my spirit by fulfilling our lifelong dreams of breeding our own herd.

Andi and I struggled in our communication and worked at practicing what we preached while facilitating clients. We specialized in communication workshops with the horses, where I developed some specific programs based on a lifetime as a horsewoman and my training at Eponaquest. Our primary focus for one of those workshops involved building a like language between communicators. Andi and I worked on that idea daily to help our relationship, sometimes successfully. We were from such different worlds;

work and life were complicated by our personal relationship instead of enhanced. I was always hyper-focused on not giving anything away about our personal relationship around clients or her family and playing the game of her needing a man with her family members. Before I realized it, I was deep in the closet, keeping secrets again.

California and my relationship with Andi proved tough on my mental and physical health, and I was struggling. I thought I had found my voice with Andi but would allow myself to be talked into believing changes in scheduling and better communication would improve our quality of life and relationship. So, I'd give in and stay the course. I suffered from diverticulitis flares three separate times and was hospitalized all three times over the course of two years after moving in with her. I heard my internal voice telling me it was time to make changes and move on, but I refused to listen until the last hospitalization. I was determined to stick it out and keep what I believed we had agreed to in our partnership.

It was the Fourth of July when I was released from the hospital for the third time. However, Andi abruptly changed her mind about picking me up from the hospital to come home. I was taken aback and really pissed off. The pain, anger, and shock of this phone call rocked me to my core. My perception of our mutual support was shattered. The $100 cab ride home certainly didn't help matters. I had plenty of time to find clarity on that ride home, and when I walked through the door, I stated that I was moving back to

Missouri, I was done with California, the situation, and her.

An ugly, multi-day argument ensued that resulted in her deciding she wanted to explore moving there too. I ultimately gave in and agreed to explore the idea with her, believing yet again that might be the change we needed to survive and thrive. I just couldn't let go of the relationship or what I believed was my share of the business, which I had given hours of blood, sweat, and tears for. By Christmas we'd moved into a new property in Missouri with all of our herd arriving two days before the holiday 2013.

The winter of 2014 was brutally cold. I spent the first eight weeks troubleshooting frozen pipes everywhere. We even replaced both outdoor hydrants inside the barn. Andi was flying back and forth to California to fulfill contracts, so it was just me and our hired hand. That winter was a brutal welcome home and reminder of how winters could be. However, I liked being back in the area; it had become home over the years and was where many of my friends and contacts resided. It felt like I suddenly had a support system. My mind and body felt better almost instantaneously.

The horses adjusted quickly and loved the thirty acres where they could graze and play. We decided to breed the mares again to Bubba, though recently, I had noticed he was off again in his left back leg. In California, he'd had some issues in his left stifle, and they'd injected his joint. After the move, his issues seemed to resurface. Though he was a bit off, he had no problems covering the mares and with our veterinarian's approval. After breeding season, I took him for x-rays, which revealed a tear in his ACL. I scheduled surgery with a top surgeon in Oklahoma in the fall, hoping he would be rideable after recovery. We were careful to manage his pain and activity in the meantime until he could have his surgery. I had high hopes for a full recovery.

In October, he and I headed to Oklahoma for surgery. The surgeon took more X-rays and ran numerous tests, which was encouraging. Apparently, we had a good shot at a full recovery. While Bubba was on the table and I was watching through the window, the surgeon stopped and came out to tell me things were worse than expected. He shared that folks in similar situations had chosen to euthanize on the table based on such findings. My stomach turned and I became numb and tingly. I heard what he was saying, but I just couldn't do it. In a selfish moment, I chose to continue with the surgery instead of letting him cross the rainbow bridge and be out of pain. The thought of not giving him a chance felt like the ultimate betrayal of love.

He came out of surgery well, and within a few days, we were headed home without good news but a flicker of hope. I knew he was going to be on stall rest for six to nine months, depending on his recovery, but I was committed to being with him every step of the way and I was. Every day, numerous times a day, I was with him; tending his wound, keeping him company, cleaning his stall, and doing anything and everything I could possibly do with and for him.

As soon as I could start hand-walking him, I did, and I always made sure another horse was in the barn for company.

I hung out with him all the time. He coped beautifully and healed. I opted to do stem cell injections to help the healing process. After the first injection, we still had plenty of stem cells left over for a second injection and decided to continue the treatment. Sadly, that was a bad call. He had a reaction within twenty-four hours of the second injection, and the process to drain and treat the resulting joint infection was quite horrendous and painful and set him back. The veterinarian thought we'd end up euthanizing him, but I followed the treatment protocol meticulously, and to everyone's surprise and relief, 364 days after surgery Bubba came off stall rest, pasture-sound and healthy.

I'm still not sure I made the right decision, one that supported his highest quality of life, but we got through it, and I can't change the past. It was gut-wrenching to put him through all of that, but my selfish heart just wouldn't allow me to do anything differently. Choosing to let go of the safest kind of love I've known, unconditional love, was just out of my reach. Today, I have a different relationship with the idea of quality of life, and if faced with a similar situation and decision, I believe I might choose differently. After all, I now live with knowing my choices caused Bubba pain and suffering; he was never fully himself again after surgery and dealt with significant pain in the cold.

After we had bred the mares back to Bubba all three were in foal. Andi and I were both excited as the first three babies were spectacular. Mel, who was truly Andi's heart horse, coliced at six months into her pregnancy. We did everything we could, but the vet was sure she'd twisted her intestine after he palpated her. We discussed surgery, knowing we'd lose the foal no matter what, and decided the best course was to euthanize her as she would not be a good patient after surgery for recovery. A horse has to be confined on stall rest to recover, with our primary consideration being whether she would get through confinement without ripping her belly incision open. Some horses just cannot cope.

Andi was devastated and inconsolable and I stepped in to handle everything with the vet while euthanizing. I did for Mel what I couldn't bring myself to do for Bubba. Not long after we euthanized Mel, we noticed a sore developing on Gypsy's teat and watched it closely. It began to change rapidly, and a tumor appeared. We had the vet out and he biopsied the tumor. It came back cancerous; the recommended course was chemotherapy at the university. We would likely lose the foal if treated aggressively but could save Gypsy.

Andi and I had a long discussion, and I suggested we try an alternative treatment protocol first, as we might save the foal since we were well into her term. Andi agreed, not standing the thought of losing another one of the girls, and we began an herbal treatment from a company I had used previously called For Love of the Horse. They provided a customized formula of herbs that we fed her several times a day. Remarkably, it worked! After several weeks of treatment, the tumor began to change until, one day, it just fell off. We didn't know what would happen after that but continued the herbal treatments as directed. Then, slowly, a second tumor began to grow in the same spot. It stopped growing at half the size of the first—about as big as a lemon. One day, it also just fell off, never to return. It seemed a miracle to us and we were elated that both had been saved.

Gypsy went full-term and delivered a beautiful and flashy pinto filly we named Tutu because of her ballerina-like gaits. Afire foaled with no problems and we named her Twyla. That filly was fierce and confident from her first breath. When Twyla, a flashy black-and-white filly was three and a half months old, Afire, just like Mel, coliced and twisted an intestine. Andi was determined not to lose another one of the girls, but Afire was the worst candidate for recovery because of her vehement hatred of confinement.

Andi elected for surgery anyway, but two days later, we learned that Afire just couldn't take being locked in a stall and was climbing the veterinary hospital walls, literally. She ripped her stitches wide open. We made the decision to euthanize her, devastating Andi, and reminding me of the importance of quality over quantity as a consideration in life. A lesson I find hard to this day for myself, but easier to consider when it comes to the critters in my life I care for. Her foal was orphaned and weaned early. Gypsy took on Afire's foals as her own after Afire was gone, it was a seamless transition and instantaneous, as if Gypsy just knew.

Several months after the foals had been weaned Gypsy had what seemed like a stroke or a seizure episode at feeding time. She kept walking in a small circle to the right and would bump into things like she couldn't see the post or gate. We had the vet out immediately and he determined she was colicing. He administered pain medication and anti-inflammatories. We took her to the equine hospital about an hour away, who recommended surgery. By the time we arrived at the surgical hospital, Gypsy had stopped exhibiting any unusual behaviors. Everyone attributed her strange episode as distress behavior from colic. Andi elected to move ahead with surgery with her fingers crossed, determined yet again to not lose one more.

The surgery went well, and five days later I went to pick Gypsy up to come home—she was a good patient with a likely full recovery. She had been off all anti-inflammatories at this point for twenty-four hours when I arrived to retrieve her. As I started to lead her to the trailer, about halfway across the parking lot, she just collapsed to the ground and couldn't move from the neck down. She looked so confused but not panicky or scared, but I sure was. I had never seen anything like it.

I yelled for help and after a minute or two, I left her side to retrieve the veterinarian. He came running out with me, Gypsy still quietly laying on the ground, as if she were patiently waiting for a solution to her confounding inability to stand. She nickered at me when I returned and the vets and most of their staff were stunned. After a few minutes of discussion and examination they formulated a plan to troubleshoot what was going on. It was the dead of winter and cold as hell outside.

I just sat on the ground with her while the vets were trying to figure things out. It was so cold, we covered her with a blanket and waited. I sat part of the time with her head in my lap gently stroking her face as my tears dropped down on her coat only to quickly freeze. Andi had been called and was on the way. They gave her anti-inflammatories, but there was no change. I just sat with her crying and talking to her; sometimes she'd gently nicker as I stroked her face. She just seemed puzzled as to why she couldn't get up; there was no distress in her eyes.

I was there for several hours with her until finally it was decided that likely she had either fractured a vertebra or had a brain tumor, and the strong anti-inflammatory drugs given for her colic had reduced the pressure for a time, allowing her body to function until the meds were out of her system. I sat there with her head in my lap as we euthanized her, Andi arrived and said goodbye, but just couldn't stay. All the California mares we had rescued were gone, but the legacy they left in all the many lives they touched through facilitation is incalculable, not to mention five babies who would grow up to carry on their legacy of helping humans.

During our first summer in Missouri, business began to pick up in the area, and our West Coast clients found it less expensive to do retreats in Missouri. Our personal relationship was on its last breath by the following winter. Our conflict had reached its peak; we argued about almost everything. Andi cycled in and out of rather extreme emotional states, heightened by stress. Arguments shifted to her verbal attacks. At first, I would freeze and allow the vile words to pelt me like stones raining from the sky. I sought support from my therapist, reflecting on my part and exploring my triggers. Back to "The Four Agreements" per author Don Miguel Ruiz I went: Do not take things personally, do not make assumptions, be impeccable with your word, and always do your best.

That winter, we hired a friend and facilitator to work with us for a long weekend. It was the only way Andi would agree to outside help for our relationship. After all, the closet was still where she lived with all but a few people in her life. The outcome was that we both loved each other and she wanted things to stay the same, whereas I needed a different way of life. I reached my deal-breaking point, and thanks to our friend, was able to find my voice and communicate through like language. I was so profoundly angry, not just with Andi but especially with myself. I had chosen numerous times to stay, to keep trying, to bend, all to hold on to a fantasy of what could be. My determination had become a strength overused; I was my own worst enemy.

Ultimately, we agreed to end our primary relationship but continue together in business, and I moved into the basement apartment. I was broken-hearted, but it was for the loss of a dream more than the ending of a long dysfunctional relationship that had really been over for quite some time. We had been living like roommates rather than partners, and the intimacy was nonexistent. After some healing time, we were working well together again.

In finding my voice with her and stating my needs, I discovered a renewed strength that shined forth from my soul. Grief had opened the door to a renewed strength and independence. It felt empowering to make decisions and choices only for myself, no more compromises and negotiations, or begging for a never-achieved date night off the farm. Just me and my pup Cali, free to discover new adventures and spend time with friends, at least that's what I was hoping for.

The toll of my stressful and conflicted lifestyle in California and going back into the closet had been life-changing, but I didn't know how much until 2016. I had a cyst in my right breast that I'd been paying attention to since my early twenties. After a mammogram I had in the spring of 2015, that cyst had been slowly changing. The cyst had enlarged and grown uncomfortable. I went back to my doctor. Testing determined it was just a cyst, but she sent me to a surgeon for an evaluation because of the discomfort.

The surgeon reviewed my scans and said that I had three options: Drain the cyst even though it would eventually fill back up because of the thickness of the walls and thus would require more drainage in the future; leave it alone; or do a lumpectomy. I knew in my bones it needed to come out. The surgeon said he wasn't worried but would send samples to pathology to be sure. He reassured me by saying he'd only been wrong once in thirty years. I was confident in my surgeon and trusted all the tests we had done. It just seemed like something I needed to handle and get out of the way to get on with life. I wasn't worried about the surgery; it wasn't my first dance with doctors or hospitals. Not to mention I had other things to focus on.

While I was dealing with my lump and tests, my half-brother John had gone into hospice in Wichita, Kansas, about three hours from where I lived. John was from my father's second marriage and was twenty years older than me. He was residing in a small group home. As a newborn, John had been found blue and not breathing in his oxygen incubator. He was resuscitated and all seemed normal until about second grade, when Dad noticed something amiss. He was sitting across from John at the table as John was practicing copying words. Dad realized that he could read about every third word as they were all written upside down and backward by John.

Soon John couldn't keep up in school and was removed to stay at home with his mom. By his early teens, they saw multiple issues including some aggressive behavior and delusions. Dad was a social worker by that time and had tried for several years to get John into the care system to no avail. One night, Dad woke up with John sitting on top of him with a butcher knife. He'd had a bad dream in which Dad was hurting his mom and John wanted to protect her. He didn't know dreams from reality at that point. Somehow, Dad was able to talk John down and got him to give Dad the knife. That incident was how my father got John into the system, and he was committed to the state hospital.

By the time I was old enough to remember John, he

was my sweet and funny big brother who would visit on occasion and for holidays. The John I came to know wasn't scary at all. He was kind and didn't seem to notice people when they stared or would turn and avoid us on the street simply because he looked and behaved differently. I knew he was labeled retarded, but none of it mattered to me or him. I loved when he would come home for a visit.

When I got older, I asked John about being hospitalized and living in group homes. He told me all about being thrown into a padded room naked at the state hospital. He said there was a hole in the floor for using the toilet, and they would hose him down once a day. After a while—he wasn't sure how long—they moved him into a room, and things started getting better. He explained to me that each place he lived and each program he started was like another grade in school. He told me that the state hospital was like kindergarten.

John was proud of his accomplishments throughout his life. He worked a job at each program and thus was employed like the rest of the family. He had goals to achieve: living in his own home alone or with a single roommate; getting his driver's license; purchasing his own station wagon; etc. The closest he came was living in a rental home with one roommate while staff would stop by to check on them daily.

I was proud of John and all he accomplished, but especially proud of his perspective and sense of humor. He modeled perseverance in daily life, he chose to learn and grow, he found a way to be comfortable in his own skin, and he was adaptable, finding adventure in each new placement home (and there were many.) He modeled acceptance, and he demonstrated that you should value your work no matter the job and so much more. He taught me so many life lessons throughout his life by modeling the above attributes. He was and still is one of my heroes.

I would pay him a visit whenever I went through town. John always wanted to go to a Chinese buffet restaurant and then to Kmart for socks and underwear. In his later years, he wasn't healthy enough for such adventures. Pre-existing health conditions and decades of strong medication had taken their toll. When John went into hospice, he had only 30 percent use of his heart left and a long list of other issues. After he mentioned some stomach issues, doctors ran some tests and discovered colon cancer. By that time, it was stage four and had metastasized all over his body. For all his doctor visits his condition had slipped through the net.

Our brother Jerry and I had gone to a doctor appointment with him to see his oncologist and discovered how undervalued he had been, and I'm sure he was not the only one. John was hard to understand when he talked as he'd lost all of his teeth at this point. However, he always had an advocate with him. The doctor spoke to us, not John, as if he were stupid and didn't understand. I was so angry with the situation and how he was treated, I'm sure an all-too-common theme. I felt defeated in my anger—there was nothing that really could be done other than prolong his suffering. We talked to John about options, chemotherapy being one. He asked if it would make him sick and we said yes it would. He took a moment and just shook his head no. I wanted to scream in the face of the doctor to do better, be better, but I didn't.

John went into at-home hospice just before Christmas 2015. Jerry stayed nearby and was with John daily, and I would drive down on the weekends. In the meantime, I was dealing with my lump. I had surgery at the beginning of February, and a few days after, drove back to John's. I got there on a Friday afternoon. On that Friday it had been decided John needed to go to hospice at the hospital, it was time. When I got there, he had just arrived and didn't seem aware of our presence. All of his case workers and staff came by to say goodbye, each teary-eyed and grieving. They all loved him.

His case worker brought a DVD of John in several talent shows over the years for us to watch while we sat with him reminiscing. We talked and cried while watching, John in the bed heavily medicated and having a hard time breathing. When the video got to a scene where John was singing, we all realized that in real life he was humming along. We were shocked, but it reassured us that he knew we were with him. A few stories were told in jest about him and he chuckled once or twice. The hospice staff had prepared us for a long haul, that it could be days or even weeks before he went home to our dad. He was gone the next morning, only two months after being diagnosed. I was so grateful to have been able to be there with him, to laugh with him, reminisce with him, thank him, and ultimately appreciate the gift of being able to say goodbye to my big brother. Two days later, I found out I had breast cancer. I was numb when I found out, grieving the loss of my brother to cancer, only to face my own journey with it.

I scheduled a second surgery to ensure clear margins, which became a partial mastectomy. I had numerous tests to check for cancer anywhere else in the breast in case a different treatment approach was needed. I caught it early and trusted my gut that surgery was the right choice. Because of that, it was stage 0 DCIS (ductal carcinoma *in situ*); only radiation and oral estrogen blockers were needed, no chemotherapy.

The idea of "only radiation" is, in truth, really the other side of a double-edged sword. The burns after five weeks were painful and severe. At the seven-week mark, I was beyond miserable, and the radiation continued its work another two weeks after the treatment stopped. It is a brutal assault to the body intended to save your life. Early on and after much meditation, I decided not to go to war with my cancer. I decided instead to make friends with body, focus on healing, welcome the treatments with as much joy as I could muster, invite the cancer to leave my body, and thank it for the message of healing it delivered. I just couldn't go to war with my own body and survive.

I worked full-time as I went through both surgeries and radiation treatment and took a total of four weeks off work throughout the entire process. At week four of the radiation,

Andi, growing frustrated, started yelling at me about how I wasn't doing my part workwise. I was dumbfounded at her disregard to what I was going through. I couldn't fathom how she could be so uncaring toward me. I was doing my best to keep going and stay strong and all she could see was how tired she was feeling. Right there in the middle of the barn aisle, as she was continuing to berate me, I lifted my shirt and bandages for her to see.

I've never seen a person's expression and demeanor change so rapidly. She had no clue what I was experiencing, and that was true of most people's perceptions regarding me and my treatment-focused world. In that moment I couldn't find my words and couldn't understand what felt to me like a total lack of caring and empathy. I felt betrayed, and the only response I could find was to show her. In all honesty, I wasn't sharing my challenges and struggles through treatment as I could have. I carried the burden myself, only asking for help when I had no other option. But after that moment when I had realized that I needed to share what I was going through in order for her to understand, Andi's perspective shifted to a kinder response and engagement with me. For the rest of treatment and recovery, she honored what I was capable of offering in labor and work without another disparaging word.

When I researched how radiation impacts a patient's quality of life, I discovered a common issue was fatigue, sometimes so severe that it could just stop you in your tracks. Some of the best ways to fight that effect were exercise and, of course, a good diet. I didn't want to worry about cooking on top of everything and had come across several articles about personal chefs and how they could be a source of support during treatment. I figured out what I could afford and reached out to a chef. In the meantime, I shared my plan with a friend, who suggested we have a freezer party. I had never heard of such a thing and I was blown away at her kindness. My friend Dodie just stepped up and said she'd take care of everything. I just had to provide friends to invite.

In a million years, I would have never thought of such an idea or felt comfortable reaching out for support in this way. I felt so loved and supported by friends who were all more than happy to help. Friends showed up each with a dish for the freezer. The irony was I had said whatever was easiest for them to bring was fine and every single person, without communicating with the others, brought lasagna! We laughed about that and over the course of treatment, I ate every single one. Dodie blessed me with her love in action, unconditional caring and support from her heart, and I was and am so appreciative of her gestures and actions. Through her gift of caring, she helped me create a new paradigm of selfless giving and love. I had stepped up in similar ways for friends but never thought to ask for reciprocation.

I've come to realize that what I considered to be independence and demonstrations of my strength were really a trauma response. The thought of being disappointed or not supported by anyone, rejection, or being perceived as weak and indefensible stopped me from asking for help. I mean, damn, I thought I was doing great from a mental health perspective, being so strong and independent. All that just goes to show how deeply those insipient strings of trauma-based manipulation and fear were hidden within me. Those strings were like fishing line: very thin, transparent, and strong, easily hiding just under the surface, wound tightly around my heart and throat.

I had several consistencies during treatment that kept me focused on healing. I worked out at the gym to stay healthy and strong. Every day after radiation, I would sit with my dog Cali on a bench outside the door and we'd look out over a pond together, surrounded by dragonflies. I'd speak with Mom, who called daily to check on me and offer support in any way I needed. Mom was the only one I let in even a little. Somehow, I found peace in the journey, even not knowing the outcome. I had faith in my body to heal and to acknowledge the lesson, learn from it and, create change for the better, and most importantly, never repeat it. I really desired this lesson with cancer to be the only one.

The horses responded in different ways throughout treatment. Some didn't seem to notice any changes, others seemed extra careful and gentle around me, and one thoroughbred had wanted nothing to do with me. The thoroughbred had sniffed my right breast when I was haltering him about two weeks into radiation and snorted as he ran off. One day, I had to catch him as I was the only one there. He was last to be caught and put into his stall for dinner, and I decided to halter him from the opposite side, a strategy that worked. I had no trouble catching him after that, but he was still cautious around me until about two months after I completed my treatment. An important reminder of how sensitive a horse can be.

By the end of my treatment, I was cancer-free. I felt blessed and grateful with a new outlook on life. Treatment ended in June, and by late fall, I had begun looking for my next life chapter.

CLEO

WE NAMED GYPSY'S first foal with Bubba Cleo. Out of the three babies from that year's crop, I resonated with her the most. I had planned on starting her and the other two girls in the spring of 2015 as they were late to mature, but breast cancer threw a wrench in my plans. So instead, I focused on healing, and by fall I focused on groundwork intermittently to prepare the girls to be backed the following spring.

During the fall of 2015, I scheduled a clinic at a friend's place just outside of New York City near Princeton, New Jersey. I was excited to be back to teaching with horses and looking forward to celebrating being cancer-free with a new perspective on life. Several conflicts sprung up with sched-uling, and ultimately, I chose to do private work instead of a multi-day clinic, freeing me up for some much-needed adventure.

I asked my friend if we could visit the city as I'd never been to New York City, and she was happy to take me. She had been surprised when she picked me up at the airport at how healthy I looked, and thrilled to help me celebrate my good health. I had told her I didn't want to see touristy attractions. I wanted to see *her* New York, and that was what she showed me. We ended up in the theater district for lunch, and I discovered that she had gotten us tickets to see *The Lion King* as a surprise! Her dear friend was a dresser on the show, and comp tickets were waiting for us, third row, center stage.

The show was amazing! It was the perfect show to take me to as I've had a fascination with puppets and puppeteering for decades. So few people know this about me, and she certainly didn't, but it seemed one of many divine interventions and universal gifts that trip. Her friend gave me a backstage tour after the show. It was a magical and healing day with a friend.

I had so much fun, I asked if we could go back into the city again the next day—I felt like a kid in a candy store consuming the city and all she had to offer. The buildings and architecture and people fed my ever-searching eyes, the cars honking, people talking and walking, music—all the sounds of the city sang in my ears and made my imagination dance with new discoveries. I rode my first Subway and I saw so many people of all shapes and sizes and cultures going about their busy days. I loved every second and smiled at everyone. I said hi to people and they would say hi back. I consumed everything that day with such curiosity and reverence.

Day two was just as much fun—with an extra twist. I really wanted to see the lesbian bars, and she obliged. I had spent so much time hiding my truth over the last decade that I just wanted to be with my community and feel fully accepted in a safe, fun space. It had been years since I had gone out to a bar and gone dancing, let alone a gay bar. As we were sitting at the bar at Henrietta Hudson's among about five other patrons on a Sunday evening, a woman came in for a drink and sat several seats down from us. My friend started chatting with her, and I went off to dance with a lesbian couple who were reporters in town for an event.

I was letting loose and just having fun for the first time in I couldn't remember how long. I was free and single in a gay bar in NYC where I felt fully accepted and could hang out with a friend. At one point later in the evening, I looked over at the woman my friend was visiting with, and it felt as though someone lifted me by my back collar and carried me straight over to her. I asked her to dance. She was surprised and didn't realize at first I was talking to her, but then she said yes. After we danced a few songs the three of us hung out for several hours drinking, laughing and playing pool as the bar filled up. I couldn't take my eyes off her. She was like a magnet to my body, it was as if I couldn't pull away from her.

Near midnight, when my friend said we would have to head out for the last train back to New Jersey, out of character I turned to the woman and said, "I'm either leaving right now with my friend or going home with you. What will it be?" After a short discussion, the woman and I headed for a hotel. This was not normal behavior for me. I've never been a one-night stand kind of a girl, but I couldn't seem to stop myself with my new lease on life. We didn't do much talking or sleeping that night, the attraction was very mutual. The sex was amazing, and it seemed we fit each other like a glove. Our sexual compatibility was mind-blowing. We treated each other like goddesses, and the kindness reciprocated was profoundly healing and mutual.

I had been worried about being with someone after surgery and treatment. I was worried about my scars being a turn-off. I felt disfigured, but she never said a word or reacted in any way other than attracted to me. When she looked at me, I felt beautiful and desired in every way. I felt whole and by morning, fulfilled. I hadn't known how starved my mind and body had been for intimacy and connection, gentle touch, and being held, until that night. She helped me heal in ways only my soul knows.

The next morning before I headed for the train and she went to work, we decided to exchange numbers and chat again. I never thought I'd meet someone in NYC, let alone have sex with them, and certainly never dreamed that such a moment in time would evolve into a relationship and love, but it did. "New York" became her nickname. She was amazing and as driven as me. We came from totally different worlds but had like values. Two weeks after I returned home, she came to visit for the weekend. I got a hotel room to ease daily distractions, and after that we were a couple.

Our relationship was long-distance, but we talked for hours nightly. We would take turns visiting, but she came to me more often because of our schedules and my farm and horse responsibilities. She loved being on the farm and actually thought my tractor with me on it was sexy, and I loved visiting the city and all that came with it. Her support and understanding about my job and passion was unwavering, and I totally got her schedule and job in publishing, which came with some really long days every month. We were in love and spoke often of a future together.

Winter of 2017 arrived with me job hunting. Soon, an opportunity arose in Florida: a teaching position in a program at a highly renowned Arabian horse farm in partnership with a college. I would be teaching classes in an accelerated associate degree program in equine management. It was a dream come true—I'd always wanted to teach at the college level. For me, this seemed like a great next chapter.

Andi was ready to downsize, and we had agreed it was time for me to move on. The hard part was negotiating how to divide things up between us. I reached a point where I no longer wanted to fight and just be done with that chapter of my life. I agreed to walk away from what I was owed. We had agreed that I would take full ownership of Cleo while she would take full ownership of the other girls and I would start over. We also agreed to Duncan staying with the herd because he was happy and loved doing facilitation work.

We negotiated Bubba staying as he wasn't rideable anymore and was happy with his pasture and care, and Andi loved him. She was the only one I trusted with him, and I knew he would have been miserable in Florida on a breeding farm in a stall and unrideable. It was heartbreaking to leave him behind, but I knew in every fiber of my being that I was doing what was best for him and his wellbeing.

Tate and Scarlet were both having a hard time with their physical issues. Tate's injury he'd suffered at two weeks old haunted him later in life, and he was in constant pain. There was nothing we could do for him anymore. Scarlet had reached a point where her blindness had become intolerable for her, and she was frightened and nervous all the time. I made the decision to euthanize them both before leaving as their quality of life was gone. Tate was 23 and Scarlet was 29. We had enjoyed decades of love and life and adventure together. I knew I was making the right decisions, but it hurt my heart deeply—my horses and our relationships were etched deeply into my soul.

Scarlet had been being looked after by Mrs. Goat during the last few years in Missouri, and she was her constant companion. Scarlet's blindness had progressed to the point of her needing to be isolated from the other horses for her safety. Mrs. Goat had come with the farm. We had walked the entire property when looking at it before purchasing and never saw her. When we closed on the property, our agent wanted to know what we wanted the seller to do with the goat. We were dumbfounded and all we could do was ask, "What goat?" We were informed she had been at the property as a nurse goat for orphaned foals for years and they couldn't catch her. It took only a second for us to decide she could stay, and so I arranged with friends to feed and check on her until we arrived weeks later.

Mrs. Goat was so excited when we arrived with horses in tow that she leapt for joy and bleated up and down the aisle as each horse came off the trailer and entered the barn. It took no time for her to begin to integrate herself into different herd groupings. She became an integral part of our farm, moving from pasture to pasture, checking on and hanging out with each of our small herds. She would even hang out with groups of people there for programs as if she were simply a part of the team.

Mrs. Goat took a particular liking to Scarlet and began hanging out with her daily as her blindness progressed. Scarlet was turned out daily in a metal round pen inside the outdoor arena which was next to a gazebo. Mrs. Goat could often be found in the gazebo next to Scarlet, napping or just watching over the farm, as if she were its guardian angel. I loved that goat. She reminded me of the love I had for Eleven and Twelve, my two lambs. The similarity in behavior andengagement warmed my heart.

Two days before the scheduled euthanization of Tate and Scarlet, I went out for morning chores and found Mrs. Goat, who had peacefully and unexpectedly passed in her sleep that night. Two days later, the vet arrived and euthanized my Scarlet and Tate. I was there when Tate came into the world, I held his heart in mine his entire life, and lovingly stroked his neck as he left, telling him how much I loved him, bawling my eyes out.

I did the same for his mom, Scarlet, as she left this world. She was so quiet and calm that morning as if she knew it was time and she would be with her beloved Mrs. Goat again. A few more pieces of my heart broke off and went with my beloved Tate and Scarlet. So many life lessons I had learned with and from them, more importantly was our relationships and unconditional love and acceptance that would be sorely missed. I'm convinced that as the horse ancestors guided them across the rainbow bridge, Mrs. Goat was there waiting for Scarlet on the other side leaping with joy and bleating to welcome them home to the great pasture on the other side.

The day after Scarlet and Tate left this world, I loaded Cleo into my trailer, put my dog, Cali, in the back seat, and headed for Florida to start over. It was a moment filled with emotions: heartbreak, fear, and excitement for my new chapter. I also felt grief and sadness. I left so much behind to start that next part of my life. I was choosing to walk away, to move forward, to be courageous and persevere yet again and rise from the ashes of loss and letting go.

Florida came with many new things for the three of us. I found a great apartment ten minutes from the farm. It was the first time I had lived completely alone and offsite from a farm in years. Cali left behind her packmates, which were all Andi's dogs, and Cleo had never been without her sisters. So, there were adjustments for all of us. I loved teaching in the program and within a few months had taken over as primary professor and dean of the equine program. I felt challenged by the new learning and empowered and vibrant as I revamped the programming to be hands-on at every level, a fully student-run breeding, training, and boarding farm. Decades of experience and success passed on to a new generation of horse people. Mentorship looked good on me, and I thrived.

Cleo and I had our first real taste of Florida that first fall during hurricane season. 2017 brought Category 4 Hurricane Irma to Florida. Having grown up in tornado country, I know all too well what Mother Nature can do. But where I came from, the tornado response occurred in seconds and was over just as quickly. Hurricane preparation, on the other hand, can last more than a week and takes a few days to pass if it even hits and moves as predicted. So, the farm staff and I watched, waited, and prepped the farm. We formulated a game plan for the herd, which included two horses to a stall in some cases and writing phone numbers on our horses with wax, along with identification tags braided into their manes. Honestly, it was stressful and made me question my decision to move down there. It was surreal.

The clock ticked away the hours. Irma chose a path inland near Tampa. Hurricanes gradually lose their punch as they move over land, and the eye of Irma passed over us, just west of Orlando. There was nothing I could do except wait it out, so Cali and I spent more than twenty-four hours in a closet together during the storm. I will never forget the sounds of the wind whistling for hours.

It was impossible not to worry about what was happening at the farm. It was agonizing to sit waiting for hours like that and not be able to connect and find out, but staff was there caring for the horses and I knew they would do their best. When all was said and done, my apartment was fine, and the farm and horses were fine too! A few shingles blew off the barn's roof, but that was pretty much it for the farm's damage toll. The farm did lose power, forcing us to haul water for a week since the well pumps were down and there were no generators to be found.

Cleo came through the event without a scratch. I had worried and prayed throughout the ordeal that I wouldn't lose her. It was the moment the world stopped, and I was forced to grieve the very real prospect of losing her and finally come to terms with and grieve all the losses I experienced just before leaving for Florida. It was a rough twenty-four hours in many ways.

Cleo adapted well and loved being out with the mare herd in Florida. I taught riding three to four hours daily, which turned out to be the perfect time to spend with Cleo. Once I had her under saddle for thirty days, I started bringing her along with me to teach. Sometimes, I rode her; sometimes, I just sat on her; other times, I just led her around. She learned how to be in an active arena, and we got to hang out and build trust.

Six months into this program I discovered how Cleo showed affection—she was not the touchy-feely type. Whenever I would sit on the mounting block with her standing next to me, she would begin to position her nose next to my neck. I could feel her breath gently against my neck, and she would stay like that with her eyes half-closed for long periods, nuzzling me. In those moments I felt such peace and unconditional acceptance, it sometimes brought tears. It was then that I discovered the true meaning of companionship in horse terms. If I close my eyes and think about those moments, I can feel her breath on my neck, and my body feels grounded and wrapped in loving acceptance.

I began to heal in Florida. My deep grieving lasted only a few months, which I'm sure was influenced by how much everything had changed for me. New York and I continued to thrive after I moved. She would come down once a month, and I savored our time together. We had fun and easily fell into a rhythm. We began discussing our future together and what that might look like realistically. I knew I was unlikely to find work in my field with horses in New York City, so me moving there was out of the question, not to mention the fact that she continually talked about how ready she was to get out of the city. In late 2019, without any action by New York to move down with me as we'd discussed and agreed to, I reached my deal breaking point.

As I look back at our time together, I realize how magical we were. I visited her in NYC one February for a week. The weather was truly wonderful and spring-like. We ventured to all her favorite places. We had breakfast at a hidden gem you could only access from an alley entrance through a secret door; it was like entering a restaurant in a garden. After breakfast, we walked in glorious sunshine, wearing only light jackets, to McSorley's Old Ale House, where we ordered several rounds of dark and took in the regulars, some tourists, and even a few celebrities.

Next that day was a taxi ride to Ivan Ramen for an unbelievably delicious chicken Ramen bowl we had seen on a food show. Our final stop was at a high-end bar with her friend who worked as a bartender. We had a nightcap and started walking home when it began to thunderstorm, in February. We got drenched, laughing and running from one canopy to the next. We ended the night with a hot shower and even hotter sex. Honest to goodness, I felt like I was living a scene out of a movie that day. I felt so invigorated experiencing the city with her. I'm sure we were an interesting sight, her in her ever-present black wardrobe and me in wranglers and Justin boots with a Carhart jacket to keep out the winter cold. I loved walking arm in arm with no worries throughout the city, no one cared. We had numerous great days together, but that one day in February still stands out.

New York talked about moving to Florida numerous times, but whenever I would ask about her job hunt or thoughts on timing, she would shut down the conversation and say she hadn't had time to look for work. I reached a breaking point, believing she was lying about moving things forward, and grew cold and angry. I ended things, but here's what I have come to realize. I manifested or the universe aligned with us connecting, and she gave me all those feels and unconditional love Cleo modeled for me. New York gave me unconditional acceptance; she honored my path, cheered me on, and believed in me. Just as I had done for her.

We could spend time together without talking, and our intimate moments were fire. In the beginning, I reciprocated but did not give her back all those things in the end. I couldn't because I couldn't give those things to myself. I sabotaged my relationship because I did not truly believe I deserved her love. With horses and other animals, no problem. With humans, my trauma got in the way. If the other person wasn't abusive, with the familiar "wine and roses" forgiveness pattern, eventually, I didn't feel loved. The never-ending layers of trauma recovery seem unending and unrepentant.

I believed New York and I would get married, that she was it. Instead, I blew that shit up, even after years of therapy and self-work. I'm grateful for the lessons and love and truly, deeply sorry for the pain. Until I can give myself the kind of love I desire, I will not be able to receive it. That's a tough pill to swallow, but what we had gives me the exciting possibility of what I might have someday.

2020 brought with it the pandemic. The college program ended, and I began running the programming for a veteran's nonprofit using horses out of the same facility. We were able to continue our veteran programming a few months into the pandemic by meeting outside, social distancing, and wearing masks. I was honored to offer this safe haven for so many veterans and their families. The horses provided so much peace and healing opportunities in that time.

Aside from the isolation and worry, I had the horses to care for and veterans to support. I began to feel community in ways I hadn't since childhood in my little hometown. Such an interesting thing that both can be true at once—a safe childhood and sexual trauma—but in my mind, I've always been able to separate the concept of predators from that of my hometown.

In the spring of 2020, Andi called with some concerns about Bubba. He was having problems with his surgical stifle and displaying signs of constant pain and discomfort. We had a long discussion and with great sorrow and many tears agreed it was time to let him go. It took four weeks for Andi to call the vet. She just kept looking for an alternative, but one morning he could hardly bear weight on that leg. So, she made the call. Right after calling the vet, she was on the line with me. She was devastated; euthanizing any horse was extremely hard for her, even when they were in excruciating pain.

We chatted for a minute, but the call was for Bubba and me. I was heartbroken and wished I could be there for him and me. She held the phone beside him on speaker, and I spent thirty minutes talking to him, thanking him for all he'd given me, telling him how much I loved him, inviting the horse ancestors to come guide his soul across the rainbow bridge, all while crying my eyes out with my heart-shattering. Our years together were truly coming to an end, a finality I was never truly prepared for with him. Andi just kept telling me that he was nuzzling the phone and licking and chewing while I talked. I told him goodbye finally, and according to Andi, he exhaled, took a few hobbled steps away, and started grazing. It was time.

Andi said he seemed to leave his body the minute the needle went in. He had changed my life and my heart forever. Grief is an interesting emotion that visits uninvited, comes in waves, and for me, also seems to help bring life and love to my memories because of my highly sensitive emotions. My early lessons in life taught me to turn off emotions and pain; but to remember all of my beautiful moments in life, I must be willing to feel my feelings. I'll take that pain at every level to hold on to my good memories. I'm grateful Andi was there with him and provided the best care possible those last few years. He was happy and loved. What more could I ask? Andi and I shared many horse goodbyes, but his was one of the toughest.

In the fall of 2020, Andi called to share with me that she had ovarian cancer. We had remained friends, and still loved one another in our own ways, and continued to talk every other week or so. Her mother had died from ovarian cancer while we were together, and when Andi got her own diagnosis, she was scared and determined to heal. It was stage three and had metastasized and spread. I was her sounding board for treatment as she walked this path. She never apologized for how she treated me when I went through cancer treatment, but I think she believed I was the person who understood what she was facing.

She took the bull by the horns, as they say, and began chemotherapy, with a hysterectomy to come. She spoke to me of wanting to spend time with her granddaughters and move closer to them. She had sold the farm just days before her diagnosis, one moment property-shopping and planning her future with more family time in mind, the next, facing a serious cancer diagnosis. Her treatment helped for a few months and then stopped working. Her boys and a few of us who were close friends arranged to take turns staying with her and helping with her care. By the time it was my turn, Andi was struggling physically and was encouraged to begin hospice.

When I went to Kansas City for my turn to stay with her in the spring of 2021, I felt the need to do something to hold onto my hard-earned reclamation of self. I needed to look into the mirror and see me, the *evolved* me that I had become, and to do that, I chose to cut off my hair. The action of cutting my hair felt transformative, as though I had released decades of gathered shame and masks from my soul. I was releasing the predefined and outdated mask of my outward appearance that had become incongruent. The act of choosing to show up and care for my friend, ex-business partner, and ex-lover with unconditional love and acceptance in my heart was surprisingly freeing.

When I arrived, I looked at her and saw the same devastation and destruction to her body from cancer as I'd seen in my brother. It was heart-wrenching and utterly sad. She had been healthy and vibrant the last time I saw her and excited for her future.

At Andi's, our first conversation after everyone left was this:

Andi: "Do you know what's happening with me?"

Me: "Yes."

Andi: "Say it."

Me: "You're dying."

Looking back, I see that I had stepped into the role I'd played so often over the years with her. I began making calls to clients and friends she wanted to notify personally. She gave me and her best friend permission to send out a letter notifying her mailing list of clients of her shift in diagnosis. So many were surprised and devastated at the news.

People had expected her to do what she had always done—survive and bring new lessons to the table. This was not to be the case; this final lesson was about the end. I helped her write notes to her granddaughters, placed sticky notes on keepsakes designating who those items were meant to go to, spoke to her friends and family, stayed by her side as her dad and siblings came to say goodbye, and took care of her.

I was there only a few weeks, and my final few days with her were spent ensuring that all the horses would load easily in the trailer to go to their new homes. The last two foals by Bubba had not been trained to load. Andi just hadn't solved that problem, so I did. She had refused to go see the horses or allow any to be brought up to the house for her. She wouldn't talk about it, but I understood. Either choice would have brought home the reality of a last goodbye.

The last day I was there, she decided it was time, and we took her to the barn in her wheelchair. Her best friend had arrived again, as had her oldest son. Her barn manager, Emily, a former lesson student of mine, brought each horse to her one by one while I remained by her side as she sat in the aisle in her wheelchair. I watched and held space for my friend in this moment, both touched and saddened. It was truly profound, and the horses were all so gentle and loving with her. It was her last goodbye to each horse, and I was honored to have been a part of that process.

Andi crossed the rainbow bridge within a few weeks of that moment. I still catch myself wanting to call her and share something that occurred with my horses or a client, to debrief an experience, just to catch up. And then I remember there's no one there to answer.

I learned a valuable lesson or two from my experience with Andi at the end. Truly honoring someone else's journey and how they choose to navigate their path must come with unconditional acceptance of their autonomy. There is no room for judgment. Whether I agreed with her choices or not, it was my place to be present and support her. We spent so much time together facilitating consensus. What an honor to live that practice to the very end. I still grieve her loss.

I was able to give her what she never seemed able to give me: unconditional acceptance and support. I was able to be there for her in the end much like I have for so many horses. The difference this time was that I got to have the actual conversations, it wasn't one-sided. She modeled a ferocity in autonomy and choice that has been a profound lesson for me. "My body, my choice" means exactly that in every way possible. Not simply in an overly independent, trauma-driven way, but in a true, self-loving and worthy of my choices in life way.

All the horses went to their perfect homes. I was not in a position to take all the girls, and the woman who did kept them together, and they still do the work. Duncan went to a brilliant therapist who works with first responders and veterans, and he is happy and healthy.

In early 2022, not even a year after Andi passed, I moved back to Kansas City to be near my mom. Covid's devastation of life influenced my decision. My time with Andi reminded me we cannot get time back, and I'm grateful I chose to be closer to Mom and nearer to the place where I grew up. My time in Florida had come to a natural end. The non-profit I was with changed direction, and my reason for staying no longer existed. On a sunny day in February, I arrived back home where I belong.

LESSONS

LOOKING BACK ON MY JOURNEY through life at this juncture, I can see the distinct colors of the threads within my tapestry. The hues of browns, blacks, umber reds, and gold that represent the horses in my life. Grounded, strong lines of strength and empowerment. Grays of many hues create shadows and veils hiding secrets of my past, secrets throughout my life that I was trained to hold but were never mine to keep. Secrets that eroded and diminished my light. Today my tapestry is bold with ever-changing and vibrant colors, and I'm grateful. Releasing these secrets into the world has allowed me to break the shackles I no longer choose to wear.

Today, I still live in Kansas City with my mom and two dogs. Cleo is with me, and we share as much time together as we possibly can. When I arrived in back here in 2022, I gifted myself time to heal, especially physically—a full year, time I would have never taken for myself before.

I published my first book, an illustrated story featuring Gypsy, *Through the Eyes of a Horse*. To pay the bills, I began driving a fuel tanker, often to the surprise of customers seeing a woman do the job. I have recently returned to the field of horses helping humans, stepping into the role of executive director for a therapeutic riding non-profit and filling my being with my favorite purpose, helping others through horses.

As I look back at patterns and threads, the constant has been hidden shame, anger, fear, and pain, but that's not the whole picture. Looking at the past from multiple angles, I recognize there is more. Many of my relationships were with women who had also experienced sexual trauma in their lives.

Throughout my years as a facilitator, I've witnessed numerous women who've shared this fact. Many friends have also shared that they experienced sexual trauma at some point. I've researched the staggering statistics on RAINN (Rape, Abuse & Incest National Network):

- 1 out of every 6 American women has been the victim of an attempted or completed rape in her lifetime.
- As of 1998, an estimated 17.7 million American women had been victims of attempted or completed rape.
- Every sixty-eight seconds an American is sexually assaulted.

You can read the article, "Victims of Sexual Violence: Statistics" and learn more about RAINN, which offers a number to call for those seeking help, here: www.rainn.org/statistics/victims-sexual-violence.

(Please note that the above statistics for this article were originally drawn from the National Institute of Justice & Centers for Disease Control & Prevention, Prevalence, Incidence and Consequences of Violence Against Women Survey (1998). The article on RAINN's website also includes the following: "The statistic listed presents information on the total number of male and female victims in the United States, using a study from 1998. Because the U.S. population has increased substantially since then, it is probable that the number of victims has as well. RAINN presents this data for educational purposes only and strongly recommends using the citations to review any and all sources for more information and detail.")

I have chosen to take a stand, raise my voice, and be a part of making the world safer. When I look at photos of myself at age six, I tell her that we will grow to stand up for ourselves and others. Horses still give me strength and courage to not only survive but also thrive. I am woman, hear me roar—I am mare, hear me nicker. The lessons horses have modeled for me, I continue to absorb and embody.

Horses are congruent; they do not wear a mask. If they are angry and need to set a boundary, they do. If they are happy, they celebrate. If they are playful, they run and buck. If there is a threat, they move to a position of safety. And they always go back to grazing, just being present and content right here, right now.

Horses are connected and in relationship. They do not do well alone. They are healthiest in a community, and so are humans when within a safe environment. Extreme independence does not mean happy and healthy; it means, *I do not feel safe relying on others because I have been victimized by other humans when I was most vulnerable.* I was not protected by my community, my herd, and so, for years, I chose to stand alone. Today, thanks to therapy and lessons from the horses, I find it easier to choose to be with a community, and when I need alone time, I no longer shame myself for needing that break, knowing it is just a break.

Horses do not spend time thinking about what happened to them yesterday or what tomorrow may bring. They savor the present moment, being with their companions, and having grass to graze or hay to eat, time with their human or herd, water, and shelter. If their needs are met, horses are good. I am getting better at this practice, and I do mean practice. Years of human training in looking back to learn lessons and forward to set goals all the time robbed me of a present state of being. So, I practice being present; some days and moments are easier than others. But when I'm with the horses, it is not hard at all to simply exist and be with them, contented.

Life has hard moments, with loss and lessons for us all. I look back at my younger self and wonder how I found such resilience, but I believe much of it came from the horses. The joy and love I found in myself and for myself with Franco, Wendy, Mischief, Chief, KingBee, Scarlet, Tate, Bubba, Cleo, and all the other horses who have crossed my path have given me life and purpose. I not only help myself through horses, but I have also had the privilege of helping others, and now I choose to help even more.

If you resonate with my story, I hope you will raise your voice with me. If you have been victimized, I hope you will raise your voice with me. If you know someone who has been the victim of sexual assault, I hope you will raise your voice with me. With my programs and my horses, I will be a part of the change I want to bring to the world and the safety I deserved as a child.

To you, I would like to say this: Take the opportunity to meet a horse, to be loved by a horse, to offer love to a horse, and feel the winds of change gently blow you in a new direction. A direction where community matters. Where difference is welcomed. Where safety from assault is commonplace. Where no other child has to carry secrets like mine. Horses changed my life for the better, and it started when I was a little girl. Just imagine what they might do for you or your child.

RESOURCES

Equine programs are available to support humans around the world. Here are a few U.S. organizations where you can find a place to meet a horse, receive support, or volunteer.

• **Path International, www.pathintl.org**
Professional Association of Therapeutic Horsemanship International (PATH Intl.) is committed to the advancement of equine-assisted services for lifelong impact.

• **Eponaquest, www.eponaquest.com**
Eponaquest, LLC is a multi-disciplinary educational organization where humans, horses and other animals are supported in co-creating a new way of being, one that emphasizes authenticity, collaboration, and experimentation.

• **EAGALA: Equine-Assisted Psychotherapy, www.eagala.org**
Eagala is dedicated to revolutionizing mental health treatment by incorporating the profound and therapeutic presence of horses. Their mission is to train and certify licensed Mental Health Professionals and qualified Equine

Specialists, enabling them to collaborate and offer an innovative form of therapy.

- **Polyvagal Equine Institute (PVEI), https://polyvagalequineinstitute.com**
Polyvagal Equine Institute is dedicated to supporting and furthering the polyvagal principles of safety through interacting, connecting, and learning from horse/human bonds.

Sexual Assault and Mental Health Resources

- **National Sexual Assault Hotline: 1-800-656-HOPE (4673)** Operated by RAINN, the nation's largest anti-sexual violence organization, https://rainn.org/resources.

- **National Sexual Violence Resource Center (NSVRC), https://www.nsvrc.org**
NSVRC) is the leading nonprofit in providing information and tools to prevent and respond to sexual violence.

- **988 Suicide & Crisis Hotline, https://988lifeline.org**
Call, text, or chat with a 988 Lifeline counselor for help during difficult moments anytime, day or night.

- **Crisis Text Line, www.crisistextline.org**
Text HOME to 741741 to get connected with a volunteer crisis counselor.

- **Safe Helpline, https://www.safehelpline.org**
Safe Helpline is the Department of Defense's (DoD) sole hotline for members of the DoD community affected by sexual assault. Find support through 1-877-995-5247.

MY TOOLBOX

I WOULD BE REMISS if I left out of my story my personal toolbox. I have had a lifelong internal drive to grow and heal. To find a way to be whole, healed, and healthy inevery way possible. I want to wake up with a smile as I hear the birds singing at the break of dawn, celebrating another day of life joyously. But here's the deal, I do not wake up every day automatically succeeding in this mindset. Just like every being on this planet, I have good days and bad days, and there have been times in my life when the bad days significantly outnumbered the good. I'd like to share the most significant tools I have acquired to support my mental health and my recovery, that I keep in my personal toolbox and use on a daily basis.

Mindset

From as far back as I can remember, perseverance has been a key component. This mindset for me has always been really simple. I just never knew or acknowledged there was another option. No matter what, I have believed in and ultimately chosen to focus on getting to the other side of my pain. Every day, the sun will rise, whether I'm here or not, and I cannot stand the idea of not seeing that next sunrise for as long as possible.

I pack my mind with all the love I can muster. That love has come in the form of Franco and Geronimo and Wendy and Chief and my mom and my dad; my friends and I thundering across the western Kansas plains; going swimming and riding my bicycle and my motorcycle and laughing… This list sounds like a child's list because that is when it began. In spite of horrific events, I found a way to focus on love, and I still use this childlike focus and belief to help me get up and get on with life whenever I need it. I don't know where it came from or how it came to be, but I am damn grateful. My pain, albeit at times horrendous, has been a stepping stone instead of the Great Wall. The love and acceptance of my animals, especially the horses, has been a keystone to thriving after surviving.

Goal-setting

Goal-setting drove me in my early years, especially my teens. I discovered the power of wearing the cape of the underdog. We had no money growing up. We grew our food, both plant and animal, because it was necessary. I knew how to slaughter chickens and rabbits before I started school. It was of the utmost importance to my father that I knew how to survive no matter what, and he taught me exactly that—how to survive. A key component to that mindset was goal-setting. Looking forward and determining what steps were needed to climb up and out of mediocrity and shine, to thrive.

This is where goal-setting began to take hold. If I wanted

to become a college graduate and a top horse trainer, I had to formulate a way to get there through goals and achievements. The first goal I remember setting was Wendy and I improving and winning at the county fair. That goal gave me hope and focus, fed by my love for everything horse, and becoming a better horsewoman. I succeeded through curiosity and experimentation with my horses. My success was always in partnership with a horse in those formative years. My goals gave me a reason to get up every day and strive to get better. Each goal was stacked upon a success, and each attempt, whether success or failure, told me which direction to go with my skills development and learning. I lived a life of failing forward, and I know having support from and being cheered on by my parents was an integral part of my ability to persevere and achieve my goals.

Acceptance and Community

Acceptance allowed me to find myself and continues to do so. The horses offer unconditional acceptance. Not once did a horse ever turn away from me based on my clothing, my hair, my age, my size, my intellect, my mood, my tears, my pain. None of it. The horses always welcomed me into their hearts and their herd because, and much to the chagrin of peers over the years, my authenticity. I was different, I have always been different, and the herd never cared. There were kids and adults who tried to bully and shame me, I have memories of teachers making fun of me in class, and those moments came with emotional pain and confusion. I took those words in only to find how to eventually spit them back out again with fire and profanity.

I embraced my invisibility in those environments simply to get through them and to the other side of my day, so I could get to my horses. They were my community, my place of respite and acceptance. I could remove my invisibility cloak and be my true self. Eventually, after leaving home, I began to find community in other like-minded humans, beginning in college and expanding around the globe throughout life. I found them because of our mutual love of horses and continue to expand my herd. I found acceptance because of who I am, in all my unique differences, because I found a way to stay open to possibility, love, and acceptance of others. Just like the horses modeled, gifted, and taught me.

Therapy and Counselling

Talk therapy entered the picture early in my college years. All of my traumas needed to come out, the stories told, and I needed to be heard by a human, not just a horse. I needed the hard conversations, to be actively heard and seen, and acknowledged. It took me a few tries to find the right therapist, and I'm so grateful my hardheadedness won and I kept looking until I found the right one. So many folks try it once and give up because it's not the right fit.

It can take time and effort to try on different therapists, to acknowledge you don't feel safe or heard by one, to keep looking for and trying new ones until the right one comes along. I persevered through the process, I was driven internally to heal, and just kept getting up and trying again and again. I wanted more time with my horses and to achieve my goals with my horses, and quite simply that kept me going and trying. I failed forward seeking the right therapist, I kept a list of what worked and felt safe and what didn't, narrowing down my needs, likes, and dislikes. Ultimately, this diligence helped me find the one I could talk to and begin a different kind of healing with.

Reading

Personal growth work caught my attention early on through a conversation with a friend, and I discovered a new genre of books, of work I could explore by myself to discover and try on new ideas. Below is a list of books and authors that have helped me over the years in no particular order. Each adding new ideas, explored beliefs, and techniques. Some I tried on and discovered they were for me, some I utilized for a short time, some I still use today, all of them dropped into my toolbox to be retrieved whenever needed.

These authors and books are at the top of my list.

Dr. Clarrissa Pinkola Estes: *Women Who Run With the Wolves, Mother Night, How to Be an Elder, Dangerous Old Woman, Joyous Body, The Late Bloomer, The Power of the Crone,* just to name a few favorites.

Don Miguel Ruiz: *The Four Agreements, The Mastery of Love*

Don Miguel Ruiz Jr.: *The Mastery of Self*

Pema Chodron: *When Things Fall Apart*

Bob Roth: *Strength in Stillness*

Dr. Wayne W. Dyer: *Your Sacred Self*

Dan Millman: *Way of the Peaceful Warrior*

Brené Brown: All her books

Glennon Doyle: *Untamed, Love Warrior*

Linda Kohanov: All her books

Joey Klein: *The Inner Matrix: A Guide to Transforming Your Life and Awakening Your Spirit*

Abraham Hicks: All his books

Karla McLaren, M.Ed.: *Emotional Genius: Discovering the Deepest Language of the Soul*

Each author or book title came into my life in a universally timed way. I was introduced by a mentor or a friend at a time I needed their teachings. From each I have taken significant learning, and I am so grateful their wisdom has been available to me and those I have passed said wisdom on to. This list is by no means a complete list, simply a list of some of my favorite books and authors who have had a significant and profound impact on me.

Meditation

Meditation has been an ongoing and powerful exploration of connection with self. Over the years I have tried numerous types of meditation. What I've learned is that my meditation practice must be fluid and diverse. I do not resonate with practicing the exact same type of meditation day in and day out. My curiosity drives me to continue to explore different types so I'm including what I like to practice below. Meditation is like therapy: it takes time and practice to find what works for each individual and that means trying different things. I don't buy into the idea of clearing the mind of all thought; I find it impossible and look to meditation practices that support my needs. I have found that there is no one true single right answer, only diversity. I am so grateful that this is true because I'm not like anyone else, so why should my meditation practice be?

TM or Transcendental Meditation is a practice developed by Maharishi Mahesh Yogi. His life's work was to revive and demystify traditional Vedic knowledge through the lens of modern science. TM has been touted by numerous people and celebrities. TM is taught through the non-profit Maharishi Foundation by trained instructors, and this is how you learn the TM technique. TM is known to provide deep rest during meditation. I utilize TM and go through cycles when I use it frequently and then cycle out into another practice. One of the benefits of going through their training is that once you've completed your initial sessions, you are a lifetime member and can refresh your practice with an instructor anytime you desire for free.

Guided meditations can be great when I'm feeling distracted and need a bit of help. The other great thing about guided meditation is that I can find a session that addresses a specific topic I want for my guided experience. There are numerous guided meditation books, websites, and apps. YouTube is a great place to find an array of guided meditations. I look for several things in a guided meditation; the presenter's voice and rhythm is important and needs to resonate with my calming energy frequency, The length of the meditation is important for me and I prefer a guided meditation that lasts twenty to thirty minutes, background sounds if any must not be distracting, and the presenter must be reputable.

Body scans are a form of guided meditation and there are numerous types of body scans available both guided and self-guided. I practice a body scan that I have developed from my learning at the Epona Center with Linda Kohanov. The version I have practiced almost daily is a very condensed check-in version shortened from the long form taught. One of the great things about a practice is that I have the ability to adjust forms and techniques to fit my needs and my world. I teach this specific activity in my workshops and private clients' sessions as a foundational practice for beginners through advanced participants. It's hard to go wrong when you dialogue with your own body.

Active meditation is another type I practice often. I utilize mantras and a check-in with my body as I walk my dogs. I find it to be a great way to connect with myself and align to my day through movement. I sometimes will repeat a single mantra day after day. Other times, I mix and match my focus and mantras to fit the day. A mantra is a word or phrase intended to deepen one's connection to self, train and focus the mind, and relax the body. A mantra example is "I am healthy, happy and whole; I choose to be present in my body today; I choose to be kind with myself, in turn being kinder to others; I am love embodied."

Joey Klein wrote the book *The Inner Matrix,* which includes several types of guided meditation. He provides trainings around the country and through licensed instructors that teach his unique approach to personal growth, which include powerful guided meditations. I have taken his classes and utilize his teachings.

When it comes to meditation, the sky is the limit. There are numerous practices I have tried and just did not resonate with at the time. The beauty of that and a curious open mind is that I can always go back, take them out of the toolbox, dust them off and try them again whenever I like. I never know when it might be time to pick up a different practice based on where I'm at in my life. What didn't resonate in my twenties could very easily resonate with me today several decades later. I never throw away my tools, I just keep the frequently used tools near the surface and can always reach deep within when I need something else or explore something completely new.

Equine Facilitated Learning & Therapy

The specific type of equine facilitated learning I practice is grounded in The Epona Approach. I am an advanced approved instructor in this technique. There are several ground-based formats that I provide clients with horses: "Heart's desire" is a guided experience with a horse where the client is guided, through body scans, to connect with their heart and engage in a sort of dialogue with their heart to determine a heart's desire with a specific horse. Another practice is utilizing the body scan facing away from a horse noticing how you feel in your body, turning to face the horse and noticing any changes in body sensations, then asking if the sensation is your own. What doesn't belong shifts and dissipates.

These are two of the practices that I provide clients and practice myself. Each are designed to enhance communication with self and the body, releasing what isn't ours, and enhancing empathy for others. These have been great tools of self-awareness and in a sense learning to use my body and senses much like a tuning fork. These are just two of several formats available through the Epona Approach.

Understanding my nervous system, more specifically fight or flight, was triggered by working with my horses. I have often preferred sensitive mounts, horses who I could build a refined and whisper-like language with, some of which have been hypervigilant in their sensitivity. I realized with Cleo, seeking to help her become more grounded and responsive instead of reactive when stimulated, that it is I who needs the work before I can help her. Because of mirror neurons, we feed off one another.

Many people have heard that horses mirror us and take that literally, but what is occurring is mirror neurons are activating in the horse's nervous system and they are picking up on our nervous system, our energetic and physical manifestation of our emotions, feelings, and our nervous system. This phrase is often used when folks are using the horse as a tool, but it works at a multitude of levels and energy moves reciprocally. If I want my horse to experience calm, I have to embody calm authentically. I realized I needed to do more work on me. I can't teach the horse to not be distracted by outside stimuli if I am constantly noticing outside stimuli.

Polyvagal Theory developed by Dr. Stephen Porges, in simplest terms, describes three stages of the autonomic nervous system: ventral vagal state where we allow connection and socialization without fear, sympathetic state where we react to stress, and the dorsal vagal state which we associate with immobilization: fight, flight, or freeze responses. Each individual has their own filters and sensitivities that enact with our vagus nervous system based on our personal life experiences, traumas, and belief systems.

I chose to work with Dr. Rebecca Bailey and her team at the Polyvagal Equine Institute where I could study polyvagal theory through experiential learning, not only to support my own growth, but also to bring to my clients, both human and horse.

EMDR Therapy

EMDR, or Eye Movement Desensitization and Reprocessing, came next. EMDR is a psychotherapy process that essentially releases blocks in the nervous system from traumatic events. I experience those blocks as trauma-based moments, like sexual assault, that have stayed frozen in my memories, psyche, and body. Moments that have stopped frozen in time that activate or illicit specific responses in my being. Diving into those "stories", looking at them from every direction possible, and utilizing EMDR to help each stuck experience begin to move has been powerful for me.

The process releases the event and allows the memory to be freed within the nervous system and to be integrated and healed. I have been able to shift my beliefs and self judgement around trauma stories and in so doing adjust my vagal response and activations. I guess in simplest terms I'm able to maintain a ventral vagal state or when activated, return to a ventral vagal state fairly quickly. I can now help my horse through mirror neurons and my authentic state of calm by embodying it with her. I can be the grounding safe energy for her to turn to in those moments she needs support or is experiencing hypervigilance. EMDR is a powerful and deep experience that should be taken seriously and practiced with a trained professional. I cannot emphasize enough that it is vitally important to find a qualified practitioner that you resonate with and feels safe with in every way.

There are so many options available to us in this day and age. Our access to ideas and models is vast because of the internet. This also means that fraudulent practitioners and untested models are prevalent. I encourage everyone to seek with a curious and open mind, be vigilant in researching the science behind the model and the practitioner, validate the information found, and be skeptical until satisfied with the authenticity and facts. Ask as many questions as possible. Trust your gut and intuition. And remember, referrals from a friend or colleague with like-minded values and beliefs can be a great place to start and explore.

These are my tools that I wanted to share with you, ways I have helped myself. This book is all about my life experiences and how I have and continue to heal. I hope you find in my transparency and sharing a curiosity to discover what might work for you on your journey. As I often say in my workshops, "I'm not asking you to change your mind or beliefs, I'm simply asking you to try on something new. New learning and experiences, possible tools, that you can do with what you like. Keep what works and leave the rest behind. Just be open to possibility."

Acknowledgements

Throughout my life, there have been steadfast lights guiding me. They were there to call me back onto my path, sometimes ever so gently and, at times, with a shockingly abrupt jolt. These acknowledgements can never list all the souls who have touched my life, but I would like to acknowledge those who have impacted me throughout the process of writing *Because of My Horse.*

My late father, Howard Huddleston, who believed in my gifts and potential as a human, and unflinchingly taught me all the lessons he could in the first twenty-six years of my life. I miss our conversations and debates.

My mother, Roberta Huddleston, dreamed of a daughter who wore dresses and loved to shop. But instead she got me, a boots and ball cap cowgirl with ferocity and fire. Thank you for setting your dreams aside for me and encouraging my actual dreams.

Brother Jerry, who has ALWAYS had my back.

Brother John, I was always your baby sister, and you were a teacher and hero to me my entire life. I miss you and hope you are adventuring about somewhere in the stars with Dad.

Donna Helmbold, thank you for modeling true authenticity, grace, and courage.

To my Eponaquest peers, it is an honor to walk this path with you. Kathleen Barry Ingram, Linda Kohanov, Eve Lee,

Ruth Le Cocq, Sue Smades, David Sonatore, Karen Head, and the late Andi Burgis — thank you for all our shared lessons with the horses, laughter, and tears.

To Rebecca Bailey, PhD, and the Polyvagal Equine Institute, thank you for sharing the path.

To Stacey Simmons, Natasha Lee Martin, and Melanie Dallas — you either answer the phone or call back whenever I have needed my tribe, especially while diving deeply into the retelling of my story. This was a ride encompassing SO many memories and emotions that were at times plain hard to relive and write.

Thank you to my publishing consultant, Martha Bullen. I feel truly seen and heard through your support and guidance, championed through a vulnerable metamorphosis while bringing this book to life. Katie Mather, my amazing editor, you were the one I was waiting for. Katie, thank you for encouraging more of my voice and helping me share my deepest emotions. To Christy Day at Constellation Book Services, thank you for sharing your artistic vision and bringing the book to life.

Finally, I want to say thank you to the horses. There are just too many to name. All have touched my heart and mind, influencing my life in every way possible. I am stronger, wiser, more agile in every way, confident, gentle, loving, open hearted, and filled with curiosity about everything — because of the herd. And to my pups past and present, there is nothing like the unconditional love and presence you have all given me in this lifetime. Thank you.

About the Author

CATHERINE HUDDLESTON grew up on the plains of Western Kansas. A lifelong horsewoman, she has loved and learned from horses since her first pony, Franco, came into her life when she was just two and a half years old.

Abundant with curiosity and drive, she has spent decades teaching and training both horses and humans through the lessons of the herd. Catherine embodies the lessons taught by the horses in her daily life. As a trauma survivor, her passion for helping others shines brightly through her heart-driven purpose to leave the world a better place because of horses.

Catherine earned a B.A. in equine studies from Park College, and an M.Ed. from William Woods University with a focus on equestrian education. She is an Eponaquest Advanced Approved facilitator, Polyvagal-informed Equine Training Specialist, and a member of PATH International.

Catherine is the author of *Because of My Horse* and *Through the Eyes of a Horse*. She lives near Kansas City, Missouri, with her dogs, horse, and family, serving the therapeutic riding community.

To learn more or contact Catherine, visit www.cathyhuddleston.com.